U0880961

智者语录

——追求幸福

丁　云　高若天◎译

青岛出版社
QINGDAO PUBLISHING HOUSE

图书在版编目（CIP）数据

智者语录 . 追求幸福 : 英汉对照 / 丁云 , 高若天译 .
— 青岛 : 青岛出版社 , 2019.4
ISBN 978-7-5552-7052-2

Ⅰ . ①智… Ⅱ . ①丁… ②高… Ⅲ . ①英语—汉语—对照读物②格言—汇编—世界 Ⅳ . ① H319.4：H

中国版本图书馆 CIP 数据核字（2019）第 049352 号

书　　名	**智者语录 · 追求幸福（英汉对照）**
译　　者	丁　云　高若天
出版发行	青岛出版社
社　　址	青岛市海尔路 182 号（266061）
本社网址	http://www.qdpub.com
邮购电话	0532-68068026
责任编辑	江伟霞　E-mail：wxjiang1206@163.com
封面设计	刘　晶
照　　排	青岛双星华信印刷有限公司
印　　刷	青岛国彩印刷有限公司
出版日期	2019 年 4 月第 1 版　2019 年 4 月第 1 次印刷
开　　本	32 开（787 mm × 1092 mm）
印　　张	8.5
字　　数	150 千
印　　数	1-6000
书　　号	ISBN 978-7-5552-7052-2
定　　价	32.00 元

编校印装质量、盗版监督服务电话　4006532017　0532-68068638

前 言

对幸福的看法仁者见仁,智者见智。

科学家发现幸福要具备五要素——认真负责、情绪稳定、坚定决心、有控制力、乐观向上这五个特质中的大多数。

有人说幸福要具备三要素:有希望、有事做、能爱人。

有人认为幸福要给感官上带来愉悦。但是感官上带来的幸福感的特点是一旦拥有,幸福感马上就消失。物质带来的幸福感也不持久。很多人可能什么都有了,可是觉得非常迷茫。经过努力而获得的成就感带来的幸福也是短暂的。正如一位哲人所言:“幸福不期而至,转眼即逝。”

有人认为做喜欢的事会带来幸福感,只要喜欢再苦再累、花钱花时间也喜欢做。另外,做擅长的而且有益于社会和他人的事情会带来幸福感。

有的学者发现决定一个人的幸福感的是人与人之间的亲密关系。自古以来人都追求爱情和亲密关系。有人说人一生最大的成就,不是你挣了多少钱、有多大名气,而是当你生病的时候,或晚年什么都不能干的时候,有多少人在你身边。亲密关系确实与幸福感密切相关。

助人也会带来幸福感。有钱可以做慈善,不是富翁,做一些力所能及的事情帮助别人不仅给别人带来益处,也能收获一份幸福满足感。

追求幸福与获得幸福的途径好像很多,条条大道通罗马。但是也有人认为幸福扑朔迷离,若即若离,苦思冥想,不得其解。不妨听听古往今来的智者是如何看待幸福、如何获取幸福的吧。尽管他们所言也相互矛盾,莫衷一是,但发人深省,催人奋进,也许会让我们找到一种醍醐灌顶的感觉。

本书所选的至理名言不仅有关于幸福的思考,也有关于幸福的关键要素,如学习与工作、爱情与亲情、健康与财富等。我们将这些名言进行简单的分类以便于查阅。读者从这些睿言智语中能获得启示,获得幸福感则是本书的宗旨,也是编者的初衷与欣慰。

另外,本书中的翻译也可为读者提供非常实用的翻译参考。在阅读此书的过程中,领略一下翻译的技巧,获得一些翻译乐趣也算是额外收获。

徐莉娜老师对本书进行了修改和部分重译,在此一并致谢。

译　者

目　录

幸福真谛

Be happy. It's one way of being wise.

幸福乃明智之举。

Life is full of care, but there are always moments of joy along the way.

人生烦恼无处不在,快乐也总是相伴而生。

My motto is: contented with little, wishing for more.

——Charles Lamb

我的信条是知足常乐,志存高远。

——查尔斯·兰姆

We all dream of that cottage in the country with roses round the door, but wouldn't life be dull if all our dreams were fulfilled?

乡间小屋、玫瑰环绕固然是心之所向,美梦都成真,生活不会沉闷?

No one can be unhappy all the time, just as no one can be happy all the time.

无人能一直痛苦,也无人能一直幸福。

Happiness is a way station between too much and too little.

——C. Pollock

中庸便是幸福。

——C·波洛克

The single most important acquisition for a happy life is that of a friend.

幸福人生唯一最重要的收获就是获得朋友。

That man is the richest whose pleasures are the cheapest.

——Henry David Thoreau

最容易快乐的人最富有。

——亨利·大卫·梭罗

Happiness is, in most of us, dependent on having friends; not a large number, but at least one or two.

我们大多数人的幸福源于有朋友。不是有很多朋友，至少一两个。

A good conscience is a continual feast.

问心无愧天天乐。

He is a wise man who does not grieve for the things he has not, but rejoices for those which he has.

智者不为所无而悲伤,但为所有而高兴。

Since we cannot always get what we like, let us like what we can get.

不能喜欢什么就有什么,那就有什么喜欢什么。

Work while you work; play while you play; this is the way; to be cheerful and gay.

——A. D. Stoddart

工作时工作,玩乐时玩乐,依此方法做,轻松又欢乐。

——A·D·斯道达特

It's a blessing to do somebody a favor, but sometimes it's a blessing to let another person do something for you.

助人是福,有时受助也是福。

Blessed is the man who expects nothing, for he shall not be disappointed.

——Alexander Pope

一无所求的人是有福之人，因为他永远也不会失望。

——亚历山大·蒲伯

A contented mind is the greatest happiness a man can enjoy in this world.

心满意足是人生在世的最大幸福。

A happy life consists in tranquility of mind.

幸福人生在于心境的平静。

What is most valuable is not what we have in our lives, but who we have in our lives.

生命中最宝贵的不是拥有什么，而是与谁相伴。

If there is no winter, spring won't be so welcome; if one doesn't occasionally encounter the mishap, he won't taste the sweetness of life.

没有冬天，春天不会如此宜人；不偶遇不幸，幸福不会如此甜蜜。

It is an illusion that youth is happy, an illusion of those who have lost it.

——William Somerset Maugham

认为年轻人幸福，是失去青春者的错觉。

——威廉·萨默塞特·毛姆

Be young, be foolish ... but most of all, be happy.

保持青春，难得糊涂，至关重要的是要满怀幸福。

What makes us unhappy with ourselves is the exaggerated idea we have of the happiness of others.

让我们感到不幸福的原因是认为别人很幸福。

Happy are the painters, for they shall not be lonely. Light and colour, peace and hope, shall keep them to the end of the day.

——Winston Churchill

画家是幸福的人，不会孤独，光线、色彩、宁静、希望与他们终生相伴。

——温斯顿·丘吉尔

Nobody is doomed to happiness all his life, and nobody is doomed to misfortune.

谁也不能注定终生幸福，谁也不会注定终生不幸。

The pursuit of happiness is a most ridiculous phrase; if you pursue happiness, you will never find it.

追求幸福的说法非常可笑，追求幸福的人永远得不到幸福。

Happiness is a choice that requires effort at times.

——Aeschylus

幸福是一种选择，有时需要努力的付出。

——埃斯库罗斯

Happiness is like a butterfly which, when pursued, is always beyond our grasp, but, if you will sit down quietly, may alight upon you.

——Nathaniel Hawthorne

幸福犹如蝴蝶，难以捕捉；静坐等候，也许从天而落。

——纳撒尼尔·霍桑

The search for happiness is one of the chief sources of unhappiness.

追寻幸福是不幸福的主要原因之一。

It is not true that suffering ennobles the character;

happiness does that sometimes.

——William Somerset Maugham

苦难使人品高尚是个伪命题,而幸福有时会有此功效。

——威廉·萨默塞特·毛姆

There are as many kinds of beauty as there are habitual ways of seeking happiness.

美的种类不胜枚举,追求幸福的惯有方式也是各种各样。

Meditation can lead to structural brain changes thought to be associated with happiness.

冥想引起大脑结构变化,增强幸福感。

There are short cuts to happiness, and dancing is one of them.

幸福多捷径,舞蹈算其一。

Be content with your lot; one cannot be first in everything.

——Aesop

随遇而安吧,不能事事占尽先机。

——伊索

Happiness is a thing to be practised, like the Violin.

幸福犹如小提琴，反复练习方能学会。

Real elation is when you feel you could touch a star without standing on tiptoe.

不用跷脚就能够到星星才是真得意。

Some see darkness, misery, and despair in a rainy day: others, a sacred blessing from the heavens,

在雨天里，有人看到的是昏暗、痛苦、绝望，有人认为这是上天赐福。

People travel far and wide looking for happiness. Sometimes, when they come back home, they find it waiting for them on the doorstep.

四海云游只为把幸福寻，回来发现幸福等候在家门。

Like harmony in music, happiness is when every part of yourself comes together in agreement.

音乐因和谐而动听，身心因和谐而幸福。

Happiness is the absence of fear.

幸福与恐惧水火不容。

Happiness is a decision, involving choice, action, and faith.

幸福取决于选择、行动和信仰。

Don't envy other people's happiness — what makes them happy might not have the same effect on you.

不要嫉妒别人的幸福，让别人幸福的事未必会给你带来幸福。

A better definition of happiness is "the capacity for enjoyment". The more we can enjoy what we have, the happier we are. It's easy to overlook the pleasure we get from loving and being loved, the company of friends, the freedom to live where we please, even good health.

——Lynn Peters

幸福更好的解释是"能够乐在其中"。我们越能乐在其中，就越幸福。施人以爱，被人所爱，有友相伴，自由选择心仪的住所，乃至身体健康，这一切所带来的快乐都易为人们忽略。

——利恩·比得斯

Everyone has a different idea of happiness. Follow your own path, not someone else's.

对幸福的看法仁者见仁，智者见智，闯自己之路，无须盲从。

Happy people don't have the best of everything; they make the best of everything.

幸福之人不是拥有最好的一切，而是使一切变得最好。

When there is life, there is happiness.

—— Lev Tolstoy

有生命就有幸福。

——列夫·托尔斯泰

In order to live a happy life, we should believe that happiness is possible.

—— Lev Tolstoy

要活得幸福，应当相信自己能获得幸福。

——列夫·托尔斯泰

Happiness is not a horse; you cannot harness it.

幸福非马，无法驾驭。

Reframe events: try to see the best, not the worst, in what happened.

重新审视所发生的事情，要看到其最好的一面，而不是最坏的一面。

There is a connection between being grateful and being happy. But who knows which one leads to the other?

感恩与幸福互为因果，但因果顺序难以说清。

To be content, we need to experience a sense of meaning, and a sense of achievement.

感到生活有意义、有成就才会让我们心满意足。

Heal yourself with happy thoughts.

乐观是医治心灵创伤的良药。

Don't tell unhappy people how happy you are. Instead, use your happiness to help them .

不要与不幸福的人谈论你的幸福，而要用你的幸福感影响别人。

You can find happiness in many different places. In the

colours of a painting ... in the clouds above your head ... the earth under your feet ... in the rosy pink sky of dawn ... and the pure white snow of winter.

我们可以随遇而乐，图画的色彩、天空的云朵、脚下的大地、黎明的红霞和冬天的白雪。

Everyone chases after happiness, not noticing that happiness is right at their heels.

人人追求幸福，却没注意幸福紧随其后。

To be without some of the things you want is an indispensable part of happiness.

——B. Russel

还没有获得渴求的东西是幸福必不可少的组成部分。

——B·罗素

True happiness is of a retired nature, and an enemy to pomp and noise.

——Joseph Addison

真正的幸福不显山露水，它摈弃浮华和喧嚣。

——约瑟夫·艾迪生

Unhappiness is best defined as the difference between our talents and our expectations.

——Edward de Bono

对痛苦的最好诠释是人们的才能和期望之间存在差异。

——爱德华·德·博诺

When pleasure is the business of life, it ceases to be pleasure.

——Thomas Chandler Haliburton

人生追求快乐,快乐便不复存在。

——托马斯·昌德乐·哈利伯顿

Love and laughter lighten the soul.

爱情与欢笑放松心灵。

It is impossible to love and to be wise.

——Francis Bacon

爱令智昏。

——弗朗西斯·培根

Count your blessings: health, family, work, leisure time,

skills, abilities, talents, the natural world around you ... The list goes on.

——James Joyce

细数身边的好事：健康、家庭、工作、闲暇、技能、能力、天赋、大自然，数不胜数。

——詹姆斯·乔伊斯

We all have to work hard in life; but spending our leisure time creatively can make all the difference to our wellbeing.

平日我们都需要努力工作，不过别出心裁度闲暇，便可增强幸福感。

Every day, find some time to sit quietly, and look at the world around you in all its beauty and variety.

每天抽空静坐一会儿，欣赏一下五彩缤纷的世界。

Make sure to mark your life with celebrations, holidays, and special occasions; otherwise, you will find that it flies by too quickly.

平日一定搞一些庆祝活动，度度假，有一些特殊时刻，否则你会发现时间过得太快。

Be grateful for the gift of life, and cherish it; never make the mistake of assuming it is yours as a right.

对生命中的礼物要心存感激，要珍惜，不要误以为理所当然归己所有。

Give yourself the gift of peace. Learn how to become mindful of life's blessings.

让自己心情平静，学会关注生活中的幸福细节。

Ask yourself whether you are happy and you cease to be so.

问自己是否幸福，便不再幸福。

Age is a matter of feeling, not of years.

——George William Crutis

年纪是个感觉的问题，而非岁月的问题。

——乔治·威廉·柯蒂斯

An energetic middle life is, I think, the only safe precursor of a vitally happy old age.

——Vida Drtton Sucader

我认为中年奋发有为，才能保证晚年快活幸福。

——维达·德顿·斯卡德

Happiness does not give, it only lends.

幸福不会永驻。

The person who lives in their own home, eats and lives simply, and has no debt to anyone, is truly happy.

住着自家房子，简单饮食起居，不为外债所困，人生之真幸福也。

As you travel, don't forget to stop sometimes and admire the view.

身在旅途，莫忘驻足赏美景。

A flower in bloom, a cloudless sky, a child's laughter — these are the gifts that can make us happy, if we choose to let them.

如果有心，盛开的鲜花、晴朗的天空、儿童的欢笑就足以让我们幸福满满。

Happiness can see you. Can you see it?

幸福在等待着你，你是否视而不见？

When one door closes, another opens.

一扇门关闭后，另一扇门将会为你打开。

Happiness is like a perfume. You cannot pour it on others without getting a few drops on yourself.

幸福如香水，洒人香水，手有余香。

Even if happiness forgets you a little bit, never completely forget about it.

纵然幸福没光顾，追求幸福不能忘。

A man' s as miserable as he thinks he is.

自认痛苦就痛苦。

In the city, we long for the peace and quiet of the countryside; in the country, we miss the bright lights.

身居城市，渴望乡村宁静；身处乡野，怀念灯光闪烁。

Every man dies. Not every man really lives.

人人都会死亡，并非人人真活过。

When we return home after a trip, we often see our normal way of life with new eyes, and can truly appreciate the blessings we have. In this way, we learn about our lives through change.

旅行归来,重新审视日常生活,会从心底里珍惜拥有的幸福,这就是变换角度了解生活。

All joy in this world comes from wanting others to be happy, and all the suffering from wanting only oneself to be happy.

快乐源于望人乐,痛苦源于望人穷。

One joy scatters a hundred griefs.

一乐驱百愁。

Happiness is not something you experience; it's something you remember.

——O. Levant

幸福不是你经历的事,而是你记忆中的事。

——O·利万特

Joy and sorrow come hand in hand.

喜忧不分家。

If you want to be happy, live in the present。

要想幸福，就过好当下。

It is not easy to find happiness in ourselves, and it is not possible to find it elsewhere.

——A. Repplier

要在自身找到幸福是不容易的，要在别的地方找到幸福则是不可能的。

——A·雷普利厄

Only when a man's life comes to its end in prosperity dare we pronounce him happy.

——Aeschylus

只有当一个人的生命在辉煌中结束时，我们才敢说他是幸福的。

——埃斯库罗斯

Most folks are about as happy as they make up their minds to be.

——Abraham Lincoln

对于大多数人来说，他们认定自己有多幸福就有多幸福。

——亚伯拉罕·林肯

Nothing is more fatal to happiness than the remembrance of happiness.

——Gide Andre

没有什么比回忆幸福更令人痛苦的了。

——纪德·安德烈

In all adversity of fortune the worst sort of misery is to have been happy.

——A. M. S. Boethius

在所有不幸中,最不幸的事是曾经幸福过。

——A·M·S·伯修斯

The path to happiness is simple—be kind to others, relax, and be thankful for what you have.

幸福并不难,只需善待他人,放松身心,感恩拥有。

Research shows that the happiness of a close contact increases the chance of being happy by fifteen percent.

研究表明亲密接触能大幅增加幸福概率。

I had the blues because I had no shoes until upon the street, I met a man who had no feet.

我没有鞋穿,心情沮丧;看到街上有人没了双脚,沮丧心情一扫光。

The way we interpret life events has a bearing on our happiness.

如何对待生活中所发生的事情,影响我们的幸福指数。

Our genetic make-up is thought to influence about fifty percent of the variation in our personal happiness. The rest is up to us!

幸福感一半取决于基因,一半取决于自己。

At the heart of a happy relationship is good communication.

幸福相处的基础是友好交流。

If you fear losing your happiness, you must have some happiness to lose.

若怕失去幸福,注定要失去某些幸福。

When we recall the past, we usually find that it is the simplest things — not the great occasions — that in retrospect give off the greatest glow of happiness.

——Bob Hope

回顾往事，通常发现，最简单的事而非重大事情才留下最幸福的记忆。

——鲍勃·霍普

Cherish all your happy moments; they make a fine cushion for old age.

幸福时光莫忘记，到了老年成安慰。

Man is the artificer of his own happiness.

——Henry David Thoreau

人是自己幸福的设计者。

——亨利·大卫·梭罗

When you are happy, do not lose the virtue of making you happy.

——Moroa

幸福之时，莫失带给你幸福的美德。

——莫罗阿

The longest day has an end.

——Howell

最难过的日子也有尽头。

——贺韦尔

Happiness is always full of flaws.

——Annebaby

幸福总是充满缺陷。

——安妮宝贝

There is no such thing as a life of passion any more than a continuous earthquake, or an eternal fever.

人不会一辈子充满激情,就像不会有持续的地震和长久的发烧。

Happiness is a field you can harvest at every season.

幸福之田,随时收获。

The two enemies of human happiness are pain and boredom.

人类幸福的两个大敌是痛苦和无聊。

People often feel not happy now, but to be happy.

人往往认为现在不幸福,将来会幸福。

The complete life, the perfect pattern, includes old age as well as youth and maturity. The beauty of the morning and the radiance of noon are good, but it would be a very silly person who drew the curtains and turned on the light in order to shut out the tranquility of the evening.

青年、中年和老年都可以享受完整又完美的人生。清晨的美丽和中午的光辉固然好,但如果拉上窗帘、打开电灯试图将黄昏的宁静关在外面,那将愚蠢之极。

Happy is the man who is living by his hobby.

——George Bernard Shaw

以爱好为生的人是幸福的。

——乔治·萧伯纳

A lifetime of happiness! No man alive could bear it; it would be hell on earth.

终身幸福!这让任何活着的人都无法忍受,那将是人间地狱。

Happiness is a form of courage.

——H. Jackson

幸福是勇气的一种形式。

——H・杰克逊

Happiness lies in the consciousness we have of it.

——George Sand

意识到自己拥有幸福才幸福。

——乔治・桑

Happiness is a state of mind that is open, friendly, and positive.

幸福源自开放、友好和乐观的心态。

A day well lived makes yesterday a dream of happiness and tomorrow vision of hope.

过好今天，成就昨日幸福之梦，带给明天以希望。

Only on the basis of keeping fit both physically and psychologically can happiness be built up.

只有身心健康才是幸福的基础。

He who has so little knowledge of human nature as to seek happiness by changing anything but his own disposition will waste his life in fruitless efforts.

不解人性,不改性情,而要改变其他一切去获得幸福,必定是徒劳无功。

Happiness is not without a lot of fear and trouble; bad luck is not without a lot of comfort and hope.

——Bacon

幸福常有恐惧与烦恼相扰;厄运常与安慰和希望相伴。

——培根

There is no happiness without dreams.

幸福与梦想形影相随。

Slow down and enjoy life.

放慢节奏,享受生活。

The smallest things in life bring happiness—watch a flower grow, or a bird fly by.

花开花落,飞鸟掠过——细枝末节带来人生快乐。

The key to happiness is patience.

幸福的关键是耐心。

Happiness lies not in owing it, but in striving and pursuing it.

幸福不在于享有幸福,而在于对幸福的努力追求中。

Only people who think that they are happy can enjoy happiness.

——Jose Johnson

认为自己幸福才幸福。

——塞·约翰逊

If you stop looking for happiness, you may find it.

不去找幸福,幸福找上门。

Kindness costs nothing, and can bring so much happiness.

善良不花钱,换来幸福满心间。

Don't refuse to accept the gift of happiness, just because you are afraid of losing it.

不要只是因为担心失去幸福而拒绝接受幸福。

If you don't ever wonder whether you are happy, you probably are.

从未质疑自己是否幸福,也许就是身在幸福中。

The aim of all the efforts from human is to gain happiness.

人类一切努力的目标在于获得幸福。

Leave the past behind; relish the present; and trust in the future.

丢弃昨天,享受今日,相信未来。

Frame your photos and diplomas. Personal objects are not just decor, they're psychological supports, increasing our sense of self and achievement.

镶起相片与证书,并非只为点缀,它们是精神支柱,增强自我感和成就感。

People in difficult circumstances can be happy, while those who live a life of ease may be miserable.

有人身处逆境会怡然自得,而有人生活安逸却痛苦不堪。

What goes around comes around — and with kindness, it really does.

凡事因果相随,善有善报。

Only when pursuing nice things consciously, one can own real happiness.

——Maxim Gorky

只有在对美好事物的自觉追求中,才能拥有真正的幸福。

——马克西姆·高尔基

At the peak of happiness, we stop thinking. Instead, we find peace.

最幸福的时刻,不是想入非非,而是心平气静。

Make sure you do something you enjoy every day; however busy you are, find time to fit it in...

每日定要寻开心,再忙也要抽时间。

Valuing others, and being valued, as part of a family, community, or enterprise, is a certain path to happiness.

与家人、邻居和同事相互尊重,是一条通往幸福之路。

Build a happiness habit. List five things per day that have made you happy.

养成幸福的习惯，每天列举 5 件让你幸福的事情。

When we approve of ourselves, rather than always seeking approval from others, we find happiness.

莫要事事求认可，自我认可才幸福。

When we're positive, we become more motivated, engaged, energetic, resilient, and productive.

积极心态让人更主动、专注、灵活、活跃、高效。

The supreme happiness of life is the conviction that we are loved; loved for ourselves, or rather in spite of ourselves.

—— Victor Hugo

最大的幸福源于相信我们得到爱，得到无条件的爱。

——维克多 · 雨果

It is easy to see how happy other people are, but we sometimes have trouble noticing it in ourselves.

看到别人幸福易，感觉自己幸福难。

When you wake up in the morning, pause for a moment to honour the gift of another day.

清晨醒来,为新一天的来临而感恩。

If you respect yourself, you will not be so upset when others show disrespect for you.

自尊者受辱不惊。

Happiness is nothing more than good health and a bad memory.

幸福只不过是健康与健忘。

Happiness often sneaks through a door you didn't know you'd left open.

幸福常通过你无意间打开的门溜进房间。

Try to come to terms with the fact that you can't have everything in life. It's obvious, but it's something we often forget!

必须接受的现实就是人生不能把一切收入囊中。这一显而易见的道理却常常被抛至脑后。

In the long run, the pessimist may be proved right; but the optimist has a better time on the trip.

—— Daniel L. Reardon

长远来看,悲观主义者也许没错,但是乐观主义者更享人生。

——丹尼尔·L·里尔登

I can complain because rose bushes have thorns, or rejoice that thorn bushes have roses.

—— J. Kenfield Morley

我可以抱怨玫瑰花丛有刺,或者喜欢长刺玫瑰花丛有花。

——J·肯菲尔德·莫里

Life seems to go by faster as we get older. So we have to find ways to slow it down. For example, by celebrating events, going on holiday, and changing our routines.

人越老,好像时间过得越快。必须设法放慢人生,比如搞纪念活动,度假,改变生活习惯。

It takes commitment and determination to be happy.

有心幸福,决心幸福,才会幸福。

It's never too late to have a happy childhood.

享受幸福童年从未为晚。

It is the chiefest point of happiness that a man is willing to be what he is.

幸福的最重要因素就是愿意接受自我。

One of the joys of old age is knowing that you have lived a full, active, and happy life.

认为自己的人生充实、活跃、幸福是老年快乐的源泉之一。

Without forgiveness, life is governed by an endless cycle of resentment and retaliation.

没有宽容,生活便成为愤怒与复仇的无限循环。

Being miserable involves certainty; being happy involves risk.

痛苦来得实在,而幸福具有风险。

A single moment of happiness can rub out hours of misery.

长期之痛苦会在幸福的瞬间消失。

If life seems long, that is because you are not really living.

如果人生似乎很长,那是因为你没有认真对待人生。

Knowledge of what is possible is the beginning of happiness.

知道何为可能,是幸福的开端。

Happiness always looks small when you hold it in your hands, but let it go and you learn at once how big and precious it is.

——Maxim Gorky

幸福在握不起眼,幸福放走显珍贵。

——马克西姆·高尔基

Life is a riddle that we may not be able to solve before we die.

生命是个谜,生前无谜底。

One is never as unhappy as one thinks, nor as happy as one hopes.

——Francois La Rochefoucauld

一个人永远不会像他所想象的那样不幸，也不会像他所希望的那样幸福。

——弗朗索瓦·拉罗什富科

To boost happiness, watch young children play and join in the fun, if you can!

要增强幸福感，可以观看孩童玩耍，若有可能与他们一起玩耍。

Happiness is about having the right frame of mind, not the right circumstances.

幸福在于心态，而非环境。

Happiness, the thing we want most in life, is often achieved by giving it away.

我们渴望生活幸福，而幸福往往不期而至。

Happiness is a natural outcome of being able to be oneself.

能够随心，自然会感到幸福。

Whenever you feel creative, playful, or silly, you are close to being happy.

何时感到才思横溢、活泼幼稚，幸福便近在咫尺。

In order to be happy, we must first know sadness.

要品尝幸福的甜蜜，首先要品尝痛苦的苦涩。

Happiness is an imaginary condition, formerly often attributed by the living to the dead, now usually attributed by adults to children, and by children to adults.

——Szasz Thomas

幸福是想象中的东西。从前，生者认为死者幸福；现在，大人认为孩子幸福；孩子则认为大人幸福。

——萨兹·托马斯

Happiness is not a goal, it is a by product.

——Eleanor Roosevelt

幸福不是目的，而是一种副产品。

——埃莉诺·罗斯福

Hope is itself a species of happiness which this world affords.

——Samuel Johnson

希望本身是这个世界能提供的一种幸福。

——塞缪尔·约翰逊

Human felicity is produced not so much by great pieces of good fortune that seldom happen as by little advantages that occur every day.

——Benjamin Franklin

与其说人的幸福来自偶尔交的大运，不如说来自日常点滴所获。

——本杰明·富兰克林

Happiness is not the fulfilment of what you want, but the realization of how much you already have.

幸福感不是如愿以偿，而是享受拥有。

Don't wake up at night and worry. Wait until morning, when you will find the problem has got smaller!

不要半夜醒来瞎担心，早晨会发现那就不是什么事儿。

Don't search for happiness itself. Instead, concentrate on the activities that make you feel happy.

不要一味地寻求幸福，而要专心于给你带来幸福的事情。

Solitude can be a friend and guide, leading you to happiness.

独处是良友,是向导,会伴你通往幸福之路。

Happiness is curling up with a good book beside a crackling fire on a cold winter's night.

寒冷的冬夜,蜷缩在噼啪作响的炉火旁阅读一本好书便会感到幸福满满。

The sweetest moments are the shortest.

最美好的时刻转眼即逝。

If you're unhappy, don't try to hide it. Express it, then let it go.

不要把痛苦憋在心里,说出来释放它。

Happiness grows when you notice it.

关注幸福,幸福感就会增强。

Being unhappy is much easier than being happy.

痛苦易,幸福难。

To find out what one is fitted to do, and to secure an opportunity to do it, is the key to happiness.

幸福的关键在于知己所长,择机发扬。

The secret of happiness, broad your interest as much as possible and try to be gentle to everybody and everything.

——Bertrand Russel

幸福的秘诀是:尽量扩大兴趣,善待一切人,善待一切事。

——伯特兰·罗素

It is rare to find a selfish person who is truly happy.

自私自利,幸福难寻。

When you can think of yesterday without regret, and tomorrow without fear, then you are near to happiness.

回忆昨日不后悔,考虑明天不担心,幸福已近在咫尺。

Do not spoil what you have by desiring what you have not; remember that what you now have was once among the things you only hoped for.

这山望着那山高会让你失去对拥有的幸福感，别忘了你所拥有的曾让你梦寐以求。

Content makes poor men rich; discontentment makes rich men poor.

—— Benjamin Franklin

心满意足，穷汉变富翁，贪得无厌，富翁变穷汉。

——本杰明·富兰克林

Travel in hope, but live in happiness.

憧憬未来，幸福当下。

Human beings are hard-wired for love and compassion.

爱心和同情与生俱生。

Even in a happy life, there are moments of despair.

幸福生活中也难免有绝望的时候。

Simple meditation can boost happiness. Every day, find a few minutes to sit somewhere quiet.

短暂冥想，幸福增强，每日当静思，只需几分钟。

Try to notice when you're happy.

幸福之时,莫忘感知。

We strive for happiness in our lives, and when we find it, we become afraid of losing it.

努力追求幸福,获得幸福后,又怕丢掉它。

Success is not the key to happiness. Happiness is the key to Success.

幸福的关键非成功,成功的关键是幸福。

Fear less, hope more. Whine less, breathe more. Talk less, say more. Hate less, love more. And all good things are yours.

少恐惧,多希望; 少牢骚,多喘气; 少聊天,多谈事; 少些恨,多些爱; 好事都归你。

The path to happiness can be steep, difficult and stony, while the path to misery can be downhill all the way.

通往幸福之路也许是陡峭、艰难而又坎坷,而通往痛苦之路也许是一路下坡。

We all share these common needs: to belong, to experience joy, to feel safe, and to be treated with respect.

归属感、幸福感、安全感、荣誉感是我们共同的需求。

Kindness to others boosts happiness. It increases life satisfaction, provides a sense of meaning, and takes our minds off our own troubles.

与人为善增强幸福感和满足感，让人感受生命的意义，忘却自己的烦恼。

Time passes more quickly if we hurry and scurry through life. Instead, stop for a moment, look around, and enjoy it.

整日奔忙，时间流逝更快，要不时驻足欣赏，享受生命乐趣。

When you lay your head on your pillow, forget how far you still have to go. Look instead at how far you've already come.

晚上睡眠，只想已走过的路，莫想尚需行多远。

Happiness can grow from a tiny seed of contentment.

幸福可以源于一丝丝满足。

The happiness of life is made up of minute fractions — the little, soon forgotten charities of a kiss or a smile, a kind look or heartfelt compliment.

——Samuel Taylor Coleridge

幸福源于细枝末节——不在意的一个吻、一个微笑、一个和善的眼神或真诚的赞美。

——塞缪尔·泰勒·柯勒律治

You may smile because you are happy; or smiling may make you happy.

你可以因幸福而微笑,微笑可以让你幸福。

There is only one difference between a long life and a good dinner: that, in the dinner, the sweets come last.

——Robert Louis Stevenson

长寿与盛宴有一点不同——盛宴的最后上甜食。

——罗伯特·路易斯·史蒂文森

The greater part of our happiness or misery depends on our dispositions and not our circumstances.

幸福与痛苦大多源于我们的性情而非处境。

Man’s life is like the sun. In adolescence, it is like the sun on the east horizon, and in seniority like the sun setting on the west horizon.

生命犹如太阳。青春期像太阳位于东方地平线上，老年时像太阳转到了西方地平线上。

Life is a movement, whether you like it or not, you must keep pace with it. You can not live in your yesterday, perhaps your childhood is colorful and worth lingering on without any thought of leaving, however, you are not likely to come back to your childhood again.

生活在向前迈进，无论你是否喜欢，必须与它同步。你不能生活在昨天。也许童年绚丽多彩，值得流连忘返，但你不可能重回童年。

Even a happy life cannot be without a measure of darkness, and the word “happy” would lose its meaning if it were not balanced by sadness.

——Carl Jung

甚至幸福生活也不会没有阴影，没有痛苦与之相对，幸福也就失去意义。

——卡尔·荣格

People who live life to its full extent seem to have no fear of death.

充分享受生活的人好像并不畏惧死亡。

The first half of life consists of the capacity to enjoy without the chance; the last half consists of the chance without the capacity.

——Mark Twain

上半生有力享乐而无缘,下半生有缘享乐而无力。

——马克·吐温

Human felicity is produced not so much by great pieces of good fortune that seldom happen , as by little advantages that occur every day .

——Benjamin Franklin

每天的小实惠比罕见的大富大贵更能给人带来幸福感。

——本杰明·富兰克林

life is fine and enjoyable, yet you must learn to enjoy your fine life.

人生美好,令人愉快,但要学会享受美好生活。

Life is not just a journey to the grave. It's an adventure to be set out on with courage and optimism.

生命并非只是通往坟墓的旅行,而是需要勇气与乐观的冒险。

There is no greater sorrow than to recall happiness in times of misery.

——Dante

痛苦之时忆幸福才是最大的痛苦。

——但丁

Happiness is neither virtue nor pleasure nor this thing nor that, but simply growth. We are happy when we are growing.

——William Butler Yeats

幸福非德非乐,非此非彼,幸福即成长,成长即幸福。

——威廉·巴特勒·叶芝

We sometimes look back on the hard times in our lives with great nostalgia, realizing that they were perhaps the happiest.

我们有时怀念往日的困苦,意识到那些日子也许最幸福。

Everyone deserves to be happy. It is within your power to become so.

每个人都有权幸福,享受幸福是你的权力。

Happiness comes when least expected; and departs just as suddenly.

幸福不期而至,转眼即逝。

Enjoy the little things, for one day you may look back and realize they were the big things.

享受生活中的细枝末节。回忆往事时,这些细枝末节都至关重要。

What the eye doesn't see, the heart doesn't grieve.

眼不见,心不烦。

Only the one who had tasted all the joys and sorrows of life and had gone through all the happiness and suffering of the world, can really understand the intension of happiness and cherish every happy time.

只有尝遍生活的甜酸苦辣、历尽人间喜怒哀乐的人,才能深刻体验幸福,珍惜每一次幸福的时光。

Happiness is a ball we run after wherever it rolls, and when it stops we kick it.

幸福是我们到处追逐的球,如果这个球停下,就踢它一脚。

Maybe it's best to treat happiness like a deer in the forest. Sometimes it will emerge from the woods and pay you a visit. But it dislikes undue attention. And if you chase it, it will run away.

也许最好像对待森林的鹿那样看待幸福:有时它像林中冒出的不速之客。不喜欢被过多注意。你若追它,它会逃走。

There is no cure for birth or death save to enjoy the interval.

——George Santayana

生死难掌控,唯享此人生。

——乔治·桑塔耶纳

To dwell on unhappiness is a waste of time. And wasting time is wasting life.

忧伤度日浪费时间,浪费时间就是浪费生命。

When you can admire, and not desire, you will have found the path to happiness.

羡慕而不奢望便是寻到了幸福之路。

The only way to avoid being miserable is not to have enough leisure to wonder whether you are happy or not.

—— George Bernard Shaw

避免痛苦的唯一办法就是无暇质疑自己是否幸福。

——乔治·萧伯纳

Happiness is a place between too little and too much.

中庸之道乃幸福之道。

He that lives in hope dances without music.

生活在希望中的人,没有音乐照样跳舞。

Most men pursue pleasure with such breathless haste that they hurry past it.

多数人拼命追求快乐,却因匆忙而错过。

There's no such thing as a free lunch.

没有免费的午餐。

Goodwill generated happiness, harmonious civilization.

—— Hugo

善意带来幸福,和谐造就文明。

——雨果

People always feel happy when close to happiness, in happiness but worry about personal gains and losses.

人总是在接近幸福时感受到幸福,生活在幸福之中却患得患失。

A bad memory is one of the keys to happiness.

—— Rita May Brown

健忘是幸福的一大法宝。

——丽塔·梅·布朗

Happiness will never come to those who do not cherish their own.

幸福永远不会青睐不珍爱自己的人。

In each country, knowledge is the most reliable foundation for public happiness.

——Washington

每个国家，知识都是公众幸福的最可靠的基础。

——华盛顿

Willpower is the source of happiness, and happiness comes from self-restraint.

意志力是幸福的源泉，幸福源于自我克制。

The secret of being miserable is to have leisure to bother about whether you are happy or not.

——George Bernard Shaw

痛苦的秘密在于有闲工夫担心自己是否幸福。

——乔治·萧伯纳

Try to keep your soul young and quivering right up to old age, and to imagine right up to the brink of death that life is only beginning. I think that is the only way to keep adding to one's talent, to one's affections, and one's inner happiness.

——George Sand

终生让心灵保持年轻与活力，临终前依然认为生命只是开始。我认为这是唯一增长才干、增强情感与内心幸福的办法。

——乔治·桑

A man who is never satisfied with himself and whom therefore nobody can please.

——Goethe

谁要是从来不满意自己，谁也不能够让他满意。

——歌德

Sometimes, we should admit to being unhappy or needing help. If we are too proud to ask, we may become isolated.

有时要承认自己难过或需要帮助，碍着面子不肯求助，便会把自己孤立起来。

A sorrow shared is a sorrow halved.

倾吐忧伤，缓解痛苦。

Write it on your heart that every day is the best of the year.

要牢记每一天都是一年中最好的一天。

Where there is life, there is happiness.

——Roman Roland

哪里有生活，哪里就有幸福。

——罗曼·罗兰

People who always think that they are not happy, will never be happy.

——Sellars

老认为自己不幸福的人,永远不会幸福。

——塞拉斯

Sometimes we lose the key to happiness, not realizing that the door is always unlocked.

有时我们失去幸福之门的钥匙,没有意识到幸福之门永远敞开着。

Learn to be pleased with everything; with wealth, so far as it makes us beneficial to others; with poverty, for not having much to care for; and with obscurity, for being unenvied.

要学会随遇而乐。富了高兴,可以周济他人;穷了高兴,可以少操心;默默无闻,值得高兴,可以免遭嫉妒。

Contentment is a pearl of great price, and whoever procures it at the expense of ten thousand desires makes a wise and a happy purchase.

心满意足价值连城,放弃欲望,知足常乐,才是明智之举。

A happy life is a blessing, not just to the person who lives it, but to the whole world.

人生快乐是福，不仅是本人之福，也是人类之福。

The only true happiness comes from squandering ourselves for a purpose.

追寻目标才能获得真正的幸福。

Youth is happy because it has a future.

—— Gogol

青年之所以幸福，是因为有前途。

——果戈里

Life is the desire for happiness, is to fight for happiness.

—— Gorky

生活就是对幸福的渴望，就是为了幸福而奋斗。

——高尔基

If we only wanted to be happy it would be easy; but we want to be happier than other people, which is almost always difficult, since we think them happier than they are.

要幸福并不难，难的是想比别人幸福，因为我们总是高估他人的幸福。

For every minute you are angry, you lose sixty seconds of happiness.

愤怒一分钟,失去幸福六十秒。

Waste not fresh tears over old griefs.

伤心往事莫提及,浪费眼泪太可惜。

Anticipating pleasure is also a pleasure.

——Friedrich Schiller

期待快乐也是快乐。

——弗里德里希·席勒

We spend our time searching for security and hate it when we get it.

—— John Steinbeck

费时寻安全,得到安全又讨厌。

——约翰·斯坦贝克

Do not be overshadowed by the mountains all around you. Instead, take pleasure in the peaceful valley that you find yourself in.

不要被周围的高山所吓倒,而要欣赏一下你所进入的宁静山谷。

You have the right to feel happy, sad, or angry, but not always the right to express those emotions whenever you want.

你有权幸福、痛苦或愤怒，但表露这些情感不能随心所欲。

Don’t resist change — if you do, you will turn happiness to sorrow.

逆势而动，幸福成伤悲。

You can’t expect to be happy all the time. Human beings are not made that way.

别奢望一直幸福，那不是人的本性。

In the war against fear, joy is the best weapon.

快乐是战胜恐惧最好的武器。

Happiness is a process of constant eagerness, from one aim to another.

幸福是不断渴望追寻一个又一个目标的过程。

Anyone who says sunshine brings happiness has never danced in the rain.

说阳光让人幸福者，一定从未在雨中狂舞过。

Don't try to define what happiness is; instead, think about what makes you unhappy, and try to change it.

不要想着给幸福下定义，而要想想不幸福的原因，然后想方设法改变这个原因。

Being able to embrace the present, without worrying about the past and the future, is crucial to being happy.

幸福的关键就是能享受今天，不担忧昨天与明天。

Give the world the best you have, and the best will come back to you.

为世界做出最大奉献，也会收获最丰厚的回报。

Ten minutes of meditation per day can help us be happier, more optimistic, and more spiritually aware.

每天冥思十分钟，会让你更快乐，更乐观，更明智。

Don't pressure yourself to be happy. Instead, create a positive mindset: be open, appreciate, curious, and kind.

不要刻意追求幸福，而要培养积极心态：开放、理解、好奇、善良。

The art of being happy lies in the power of extracting happiness from common things.

能够从寻常生活中感受幸福便是幸福的艺术。

A child's smile, a warm summer's day; these are the gifts that make us happiest.

孩子的一个微笑、一个温暖的夏日，都是让我们非常幸福的礼物。

Better by far you should forget and smile than that you should remember and be sad.

——Chtistina Georgina Rossetti

宁愿因健忘而幸福，也不要因回忆而伤心。

——克里斯提娜·乔治娜·罗塞蒂

Happiness breaks easily, like glass.

幸福如玻璃，容易破碎。

The very remembrance of my former misfortune proves a new one to me.

——Cervantes

不能忘记往日的不幸正是我现在新的不幸。

——塞万提斯

A truly happy person is one who can enjoy the scenery while on a detour.

真正幸福的人走在崎岖的路上依然能欣赏风景。

Happiness grows at our own firesides, and is not to be picked in strangers' garden.

——D. W. Jerrold

幸福孕育在我们自己的火炉边,而非从别人花园中采的果实。

——D·W·杰罗尔德

True happiness is to enjoy the present, without anxious dependence upon the future.

真正的幸福是享受当下而非惴惴不安地寄希望于未来。

Watching the sun come up in the morning reminds us that all is possible when a new day begins.

观看朝日升起,让我们对新的一天又充满希望。

Don't envy another's happiness, instead, try to share in it.

不要嫉妒他人幸福,而要从中分得一杯羹。

People facing death often realize for the first time how much they love life. Think how that feels, and try to value what you have now.

濒临死亡者常会首次意识到对生命的热爱。设身处地想一想,学会珍视现有的一切。

We are most true to ourselves when we're about nine or ten. So revisit that time in your life by taking up the hobbies that you enjoyed as a child.

儿童时代最纯真,重拾童趣,便可回归天真。

Compassion is at the heart of happiness.

同情心是幸福的根基。

Happiness is contagious.

幸福具有感染力。

The wisdom of life consists in the elimination of non-essentials.

生活的智慧在于放弃非必需品。

Nobody really cares if you're miserable, so you might as well be happy.

无人真关心你是否伤心难过,不妨快乐过好每一天。

Happiness is the greatest gift a person can have or bestow.

幸福是人所能得到的或者给予的最珍贵的礼物。

Five keys to happier living: giving; relating; appreciating; accepting; questing.

幸福五要素:奉献、交往、感恩、接受、探索。

Happiness has magical properties. It leads to long life, health, and resilience.

幸福具有神奇的魔力,让人健康长寿,充满活力。

The art of happiness is like any other — the more you practise it, the better you get at it.

获取幸福的艺术一如其他,也是熟能生巧。

There is no happiness without dreams.

没有梦想就无幸福可言。

When you tend your garden, you also tend your soul.

打理花园,愉悦心灵。

When ambition ends, happiness begins.

野心不在,幸福到来。

Where there is laughter, there is happiness.

笑声之处见幸福。

Sometimes happiness is free; sometimes, it comes at a cost.

有时幸福无须花费,有时要付出代价。

Having achieved a special goal in life can make you happy, but there may also be a feeling of anti-climax — before you begin to aim for a new one.

达到人生某个特殊目标带来的幸福感会在开始追求新的目标前逐渐消退。

The path to happiness is a pilgrimage that everyone must make for themselves.

通往幸福之路是每个人必须亲自跋涉的朝圣之路。

Happiness is a skill we can learn.

幸福是技巧,我们都能学。

Ignorance never brings happiness; the source of happiness lies in knowledge.

—— Zola

无知绝不会带来幸福;幸福的根源在于知识。

——左拉

There are three ingredients in the good life: learning, earning, and yearning.

幸福生活三要素:学习,赚钱,期望。

The essence of philosophy is that a man should so live that his happiness shall depend as little as possible on external things.

哲学的真谛就是让人知道如何生活才能最大限度地不靠外因获得幸福。

There is no happiness without struggle.

没有奋斗就没有幸福。

One needs 3 things to be truly happy living in the world: some thing to do, some one to love, some thing to hope for.

人生在世要得到真正的幸福,只需三个条件: 有所为,有所爱,有所盼。

The highest enjoyment is to complete what others think you can't do.

——Pei de Raadt

最大的幸福是完成别人认为你无法做到的事情。

——培德·若特

Happiness is the natural flower of duty.

尽职尽责,幸福之花自然开放。

Misfortune is difficult to bear, but happiness is hard to bear.

——Holderlin

承担不幸是困难的,但要负担幸福更是难上难。

——荷尔德林

Boredom is the misfortune of a happy man.

——Walpole

无聊是幸福者的不幸。

——沃波尔

Watching a bee take nectar from a flower you've grown is a happy sight to see.

蜜蜂在你种植的花中采蜜,美景赏心悦目。

The way we interpret life events has a bearing on our happiness.

生活态度影响生活的幸福。

He who plants a garden plants happiness.

在园里种植就是种植幸福。

Happiness comes out of the capacity to feel deeply, to enjoy simply, to think freely, to risk life, to be needed.

——Storm Jameson

幸福源于深刻的感受力、简单的享受、自由的思考、生命的冒险以及自己被需要。

——史托姆·詹姆森

Some pursue happiness, others create it.

有人追求幸福，有人创造幸福。

Let nothing distract us from being happy, let nothing else determine our fate, but ourselves. What makes us happy is what matters in the end, not what we acquire.

——Olehile Fischer Thataone

不要让任何事情影响我们的幸福，除了自己，不要让任何其他事决定我们的命运。我们的幸福取决于最终所看重的东西而非所得。

——欧利·希尔·萨韬恩

Happiness is not an emotion that we learn; we automatically get it.

——Dan Baker

幸福不是学来的，而是自动来到的。

——丹·贝克

The foolish man seeks happiness in the distance; the wise grows it under his feet.

傻瓜到远方寻求幸福，聪明人在脚下栽培幸福。

True happiness is when you realize the value of life.

—— Munir Nassef

意识到人生的价值才是真正的幸福。

——穆尼尔·纳素夫

Happiness is the most precious wine, but the vulgar people, is ignorant like chewing wax.

——Lo Smith

幸福是最珍贵的葡萄美酒，但粗俗之人不知其价值，饮之如嚼蜡。

——洛·史密斯

There is no paradise on earth equal to the union of love and innocence.

——Rousseau

爱与纯真的结合便是人间天堂。

——卢梭

When you try to pursue happiness, it's often avoiding you; when you try to avoid happiness, it's often following you.

追求幸福，幸福往往逃避；逃避幸福，幸福却又常常追随。

Make a list of things that make you happy. You'll find there are more of them than you imagined...

列举一下让你感到幸福的事情，数量之多大大超乎意料。

The purpose of all human efforts is to obtain happiness.

——Erwin

人类的一切努力都是为了获得幸福。

——欧文

学习与工作

All the blessings we enjoy are the fruits of labor, toil, and self-denial, and study.

——William Graham Sumner

所有的幸福都是劳动、辛苦、自我克制和学习的成果。

——威廉·格拉哈姆·萨姆纳

If you're never scared or embarrassed or hurt, it means you never take any chances.

从未恐惧、尴尬或受伤，意味着从未冒险。

A man's deepest contentment will come from attempting to fathom what can be fathomed, and honoring in silence what cannot be fathomed.

人最深层次的满足源于探索可以探索的，默默放下无法探究的。

Times of general calamity and confusion have ever been productive of the greatest minds. The purest ore is produced from the hottest furnace. If you will call your troubles experiences, and remember that every experience develops some latent force within you, you will grow vigorous and happy, however adverse your circumstances may seem to be.

乱世出英雄，百炼成钢，若视苦难为历练，每一次历练都会积累潜力，任凭风吹浪打，你依然会精力充沛，幸福满满。

To love what you do and feel that it matters— how could anything be more fun?

热爱工作，深感重要，会让你快乐无比。

To youth I have but three words of counsel—work, work, and work.

对青年，我的忠告只有三个词——工作、工作、工作。

Who likes not his business, his business likes not him.

谁若不爱自己的事业，也不会得到事业的垂青。

He who risks nothing gains nothing.

收获与风险并存。

Do not, for one repulse, give up the purpose that you resolved to effect.

——William Shakespeare

不要只因一次失败,就放弃你原来决心想达到的目的。

——威廉·莎士比亚

Work is more than necessary for most human beings. It is the focus of their lives, the source of their identity and creativity.

——Leonard R. Sayles

对大多数人来说,工作不仅仅是一种必需,还是生活的焦点,是身份的来源和创造性的源泉。

——雷奥那多·R·塞尔斯

Happiness comes from a sense of accomplishment, from a creative work.

——Franklin D. Roosevelt

幸福来自成就感和富有创意的工作。

——富兰克林·D·罗斯福

Work is the grand cure for all the maladies and miseries that ever beset mankind.

——Thomas Carlyle

工作是一剂良药,能解决困扰人们的一切疾苦。

——托马斯·卡莱尔

Why should work be such a significant source of human satisfaction? A good share of the answer rest in the kind of pride that is stimulated by the job, by the activity of accomplishing.

——Leonard R. Sayles

为什么工作是人们获得满足感的重要源泉呢？最主要的答案就在于工作和完成工作的过程能激起一种自豪感。

——雷奥那多·R·塞尔斯

Work banishes those three great evils: boredom, vice, and poverty.

——Voltaire

工作撵跑三个魔鬼：无聊、堕落和贫穷。

——伏尔泰

Work won't kill, but worry will.

工作不伤人，忧虑却伤身。

Don't let obstacles in life stand in your way. If you can't jump over them, go round them.

不要叫生活中的障碍挡去路，或一跃而过，或绕道而行。

Turn the rocks in your path into stepping stones to help you along your way.

把绊脚石变为垫脚石，百尺竿头更进一步。

The cure for anything is salt water—sweat, tears, or the sea.

—— Isak Dinesen

汗水、泪水或海水是治疗一切的良药。

——伊萨克·丁尼生

Action may not bring happiness, but there is no happiness without action.

行动不一定带来幸福，不行动必定没有幸福。

To do great work a man must be very idle as well as very industrious.

——Samuel Bubler

要从事伟大的工作，一个人必须既非常勤劳又有很多闲暇时间。

——塞缪尔·勃特勒

Work connects us to others, building a happier world for everyone.

工作让我们结缘，共建共享幸福家园。

The best part of one's life is the working part, the creative part. Believe me, I love to succeed; but the real spiritual and emotional excitement is in the doing.

——Garson Kanin

工作与创新的阶段是人生最美好的时光。我爱成功，但真正令人激动的时候是在争取成功的工作中。

——加森·卡宁

Concentrate on the task in hand. However trivial, you will feel happier if you do it well.

专心手中活儿，做好都快乐。

Build some variation into your life. Take a different route to work, try food from a different culture, or visit a museum or gallery you've never been to before.

让自己的生活丰富多变：另辟新路去工作，尝试不同文化的饮食，参观从未去过的博物馆与画廊。

Life is the art of drawing sufficient conclusions from insufficient premises.

——Samuel Butler

生活是一种艺术，要在不充足的前提下得出充足的结论。

——塞缪尔·巴特勒

Better to light a candle than curse the darkness.

与其诅咒黑暗，不如点亮蜡烛。

Man needs, for his happiness, not only the enjoyment of this or that, but hope and enterprise and change.

——Bertrand Russell

男人的幸福并非只是需要享用这个那个，而是需要希望、事业和变化。

——伯特兰·罗素

To travel hopefully is a better thing than to arrive, and the true success is to labor.

怀着希望旅行比抵达目的地更愉快，真正的成功寓于工作中。

There are tricks in every trade.

各行各业都有诀窍。

If you have a job without any aggravations, you don't have a job.

工作没有一点压力,就不叫工作。

Jobs and work do much more than most of us realize to provide happiness and contentment.

——Leonard R. Sayles

多数人意识不到幸福和满足主要来自职业和工作。

——雷奥那多·R·塞尔斯

Finished labors are pleasant.

工作完成,心情愉悦。

You can't help getting older, but you don't have to get old. New dreams, new works in progress — that's the ticket for a long and happy ride.

——George Burns

年龄无法控制,心态可以不老,追求梦想与事业让人幸福长寿。

——乔治·伯恩斯

Pure and complete sorrow is as impossible as pure and complete joy.

——Leo Tolstoy

不存在纯粹的绝对哀伤,也不存在纯粹的绝对欢乐。

——列夫·托尔斯泰

A change of work is as good as a rest.

调换一下工作就是一种休息。

We either make ourselves miserable, or we make ourselves strong. The amount of work is the same.

——Carlos Castaneda

工作量不变,我们可以因此而痛苦,也可以因此而强壮。

——卡洛斯·卡斯塔尼达

Bringing love, luck, and happiness into your life takes hard work. It doesn't happen by itself.

幸福不会从天降,努力工作才能带来爱情、幸运与幸福。

True happiness consists in the full use of one's ability and talent.

—— Douglas Fejs

真正的幸福在于充分发挥自己的才能。

——道格拉斯・斐杰斯

Dream a big dream, taking positive action to move you onward and upward toward your goals.

——Kurt Lee Hurley

志存高远,积极行动,朝目标奋进。

——库尔特・李・赫尔利

Life is not a race, and the winner is not always the one who finishes first.

生活不是赛跑,胜者并非首个冲向终点者。

The world is like a mirror; frown at it, and it frowns at you. Smile and it smiles, too.

——Herbert Samuel

世界如镜,你朝它皱眉,它朝你皱眉;你朝它微笑,它朝你微笑。

——赫伯特・塞缪尔

Before we set our hearts too much upon anything, let us examine how happy those are who already possess it.

在全力争取某样东西时，先审视拥有者幸福程度如何。

Finding new avenues for your talents in new ways increases happiness — your own, and that of others.

才华找到新的用武之地，于己于人都更幸福。

The best preparation for good work tomorrow is to do good work today.

——Elbert Hubbard

做好明天工作的最好准备就是做好今天的工作。

——艾尔伯特·哈伯德

Business is the salt of life.

事业是人生之盐。

Goals determine what you are going to be.

——Julius Irving

目标决定你将成为什么样的人。

——朱利叶斯·欧文

Business may be troublesome, but idleness is pernicious.

业务虽烦扰,懒惰更有害。

Business neglected is business lost.

忽视工作等于丢掉工作。

Business sweetens pleasure, and labor sweetens rest.

工作使消遣更愉快,劳动使休息更快乐。

Do business, but be not a slave to it.

要工作,但不要当工作的奴隶。

Drive your business; do not let it drive you.

要推动事业发展,不要让事业来推动你。

He that will not work shall not eat.

不劳动者不得食。

When work is a pleasure, life is joy! When work is duty, life is slavery.

——Maxim Gorky

工作是一种乐趣时，生活是一种享受！工作是一种义务时，生活则是一种苦役。

——马克西姆·高尔基

Creativity is within everyone's reach — no exceptions. And to be creative, even in a small way, can bring great happiness.

谁都有创造力，无一例外。创新，哪怕很小的创新都会让人感到幸福满满。

A great pleasure in life is doing what people say you cannot do.

人生一大乐事就是做别人说你做不到的事情。

He that would rise at court must begin by creeping.

九层之台，起于累土。

It is easy to open a shop but hard to keep it always open.

创业容易守业难。

He that thinks his business below him will always be below his business.

自命大材小用的人往往眼高手低。

No cross, no crown.

不受苦中苦,难为人上人。

Nothing venture, nothing have.

没有风险,没有收获。

Keeping is harder than winning.

创业难,守业更难。

Never was good work done without great effort.

不花大力气干不好工作。

Creativity is a catalyst for happiness.

创新是幸福的催化剂。

Nothing great was ever achieved without enthusiasm.

没有热情,成就不了伟业。

On Monday mornings don't be looking for Saturday night.

不要在星期一早上就翘首期盼星期六晚上。

Only those who have the patience to do simple things perfectly ever acquire the skill to do difficult things easily.

——Friedrich Schiller

只有有耐心圆满完成简单工作的人才能够轻而易举地完成困难的工作。

——弗里德里希·席勒

Don't part with your illusions. When they are gone you may still exist, but you have ceased to live.

——Mark Twain

不要放弃幻想。没有幻想,可以生存,但虽生犹死。

——马克·吐温

Make happiness your goal, and do whatever it takes to achieve it.

把幸福设为目标,为此目标而不懈努力。

Cease to struggle and you cease to live.

——Thomas Carlyle

生命不止,奋斗不息。

——托马斯·卡莱尔

Time is money for enterprisers.

对企业家来说，时间就是金钱。

The harder I work, the luckier I get.

工作越努力，人生越幸运。

Life grants nothing to us mortals without hard work.

天道酬勤。

The greatest happiness lies in our shortcomings and our mistakes which are corrected.

—— Gerd

改正错误与缺点是最大的幸福。

——格尔德

As long as you have a reasonable thing to do, your life will be very beautiful.

——Einstein

只要有件合理的事做，生活就会很美好。

——爱因斯坦

Many persons have a wrong idea of what constitutes true

happiness. It is not attained through self-gratification, but through fidelity to a worthy purpose.

——Helen Keller

很多人对真正幸福的看法有误。幸福不是自我满足，而是为崇高的事业而献身。

——海伦·凯勒

True happiness comes from the joy of deeds well done, the zest of creating things new.

真正的幸福源于功成名就、创新激情。

Happiness fuels success, not the other way round.

幸福助推成功，而不会阻碍成功。

Success is never a measure of happiness.

成功绝非意味着幸福。

Work bears witness who does well.

工作能证明谁做得好。

Stick to it, and you'll succeed.

只要有恒心，万事皆能成。

It is no use doing what you like; you have got to like what you do.

——Winston Churchill

不能爱哪行才干哪行,要干哪行爱哪行。

——温斯顿·丘吉尔

My philosophy of life is work.

——Thomas Edison

我的人生哲学就是工作。

——托马斯·爱迪生

Happiness lies not in the mere possession of money ; it lies in the joy of achievement , in the thrill of creative effort.

——Franklin Roosevelt

幸福不仅仅在于拥有金钱,而在于获得成就时的喜悦以及努力创新的激情。

——富兰克林·罗斯福

Taking time and space for yourself will make you happier, however busy you are.

忙忙碌碌无止境,抽空偷闲享人生。

Get your work/life balance right. Make clear boundaries, and stick to them. Otherwise your life will slip by without you noticing.

工作、生活要平衡,工作、生活两分清,坚守界限不放松,莫叫人生溜走急匆匆。

Every man's work, whether it be literature or music or pictures or architecture or anything else, is always a portrait of himself.

——Samuel Butler

每个人的工作,无论是文学、音乐、美术、建筑还是其他工作,都是自己的一幅画像。

——塞缪尔 · 巴特勒

The tears of happiness can be caused by the sweat of labor; the tears of despair only can be erased by struggle.

幸福的泪水可以靠劳动的汗水换来;绝望的泪只有靠奋斗才能抹去。

Industry is fortune's right hand, and frugality her left.

——John Ray

勤劳是财富的右手,节俭是她的左手。

——约翰 · 雷伊

Labor is the father of happiness.

——Franklin

劳动是幸福之父。

——富兰克林

Business makes a man as well as tries him.

事业可以考验人,也可以造就人。

Difficult circumstances serve as a textbook of life for people.

困难坎坷是人们的生活教科书。

I slept and dreamt that life was beauty; I woke and found that life was duty.

睡梦里人生美丽无比,醒时发现人生即是义务。

If you approach work with passion and energy, it will help you to be happy.

充满激情、全神贯注地工作会带来幸福感。

Make the best of a bad bargain.

面对困境,尽力而为。

Never do things by halves.

做事不要半途而废。

Happiness, I have discovered, is nearly always a rebound from hard work.

——David Grayson

我发现辛勤工作总能回报以幸福。

——大卫·格雷森

Working without a plan is sailing without a compass.

工作无计划,犹如航海无罗盘。

Whoever is in a hurry shows that the thing he is about is too big for him.

不管是谁,匆匆忙忙只能说明他不能胜任所从事的工作。

In order that people may be happy in their work, these things are needed: they must be fit for it; they must not do much of it; and they must have a sense of success in it.

——John Ruskin

工作要快乐的三个要素：必须胜任，不要揽太多，有成就感。

——约翰·罗斯金

No man is a failure who is enjoying life.

——William Feather

享受生活者不是失败者。

——威廉·费泽

Happiness exists in a person's real work.

——Marcus Aurelius

幸福存在于一个人真正的工作中。

——马可·奥里利乌斯

To enrich your time makes you happy.

——Emerson

过得充实便是幸福。

——爱默生

Never leave the path of duty and honor, this is the only way to get happiness.

坚守责任与荣誉是获得幸福的唯一方法。

爱情与亲情

The supreme happiness of life is the conviction that we are loved.

——V. Hugo

生活中最大的幸福是坚信有人爱我们。

——V·雨果

Love is the condition in which another person's happiness is essential to your own.

休戚与共,爱情之基。

As selfishness and complaint cloud the mind, so love with its joy clears and sharpens the vision.

——Helen Keller

自私和抱怨蒙蔽心智,愉快的爱让人心明眼亮。

——海伦·凯勒

A cheerful wife is the joy of life.

乐天的妻子让你生活快乐。

To love one another is to be happy.

彼此相爱就是幸福。

Nothing is more warm than home, nothing is more precious than family.

没有什么比家更温暖,没有什么比亲情更珍贵。

Happiness is like the shadow behind you, you can not catch, but as long as you move forward, it will always follow you.

幸福如影相随,无法追到,但只要你往前走,它会一直跟随。

The greatest happiness in life is that you find the one you love is loving you as well.

人生最大的幸福就是自己所爱的人也爱着自己。

There are many people who use the happiness of youth as the price of success.

—— Mozart

许多人用青春的幸福作为成功的代价。

——莫扎特

If you feel jealous of others, take a closer look at their lives, and ask, would I really want to be them?

若把他人妒,细察其生活,并扪心自问:你愿那样过?

Try to see the best in people.

把人往最好处看。

Love can turn sorrow into happiness.

爱能化悲为喜。

Nurturing and loving someone is the key to happiness.

抚育所爱，幸福之源。

Never let a day go by without giving thanks for it.

每过一天，勿忘感恩。

Love and laughter lighten the soul.

爱情与欢笑放松心灵。

Take pleasure in the little things of life: a hearty meal; a crackling fire; laughter of friends; the smile of a loved one.

细微之处享生活：一顿美餐、炉火噼啪、朋友大笑、爱人微笑。

He who seeks only for applause from others has all his happiness in another's keeping.

一味寻求别人的赞赏，就是将幸福交到别人手里。

It's the greatest happiness in the world to make your beloved one happy.

让所爱的人快乐,是世界上最大的幸福。

If we want to be happy, we need to put love first.

要想幸福,要先有爱。

Youth is the season made for joys, love is the then duty.

青春让人快乐,爱情赋予责任。

Youth is happy, for it is promising.

青春之所以幸福,是因为充满希望。

Happiness is an activity, not an emotion.

幸福源于行动而非情感。

Darkness cannot drive out darkness; only light can do that. Hate cannot drive out hate; only love can do that.

——Martin Luther King

黑暗不能驱赶黑暗,只有光明能够做到。仇恨不能赶走仇恨,只有爱能够做到。

——马丁·路德·金

Yearning others is warmth while being yearned is happiness.

思念是温暖，被思念是幸福。

The happiness of a man does not consist in the absence but in the mastery of his passions.

男人的幸福不能没有激情，又要掌控激情。

Love one another but make not a bond of love: let it rather be a moving sea between the shores of your souls.

相爱但不相互约束，让爱成为大海在两个心灵海岸之间激荡。

Happiness is the spiritual experience of living every minute with love, grace, and gratitude.

幸福便是时刻感受爱意、优雅与感恩。

There is only one happiness in life, to love and be loved.

—— George Sand

人生只有一种幸福，就是爱和被爱。

——乔治·桑

Happiness is a way of life, an overriding outlook

composed of qualities such as optimism, courage, love, and fulfillment. It's not something that changes every time your situation changes.

——Dan Baker

幸福是一种生活方式,主张乐观、勇敢、爱以及成就等,这种主张并不随着处境的改变而改变。

——丹·贝克

To be happy, you need to know that others love you for yourself, just as you are.

要想幸福,需要知道别人真心爱你,就像你爱别人一样。

The family should be the palace of love, joy and laughter.

家庭应该是爱、快乐和欢笑的殿堂。

Only love is stronger than death.

——Samuel Johnson

只有爱比死亡强大。

——塞缪尔·约翰逊

What matters most in parenting is not strict routine, but

providing unconditional love for children and helping them to feel understood, valued, and secure.

做父母,最重要的并非严格管教,而是无条件地爱孩子,帮孩子感受到父母的理解、尊重与保护。

I cannot think of any need in childhood as strong as the need for a father's protection.

——Sigmund Freud

我认为人在童年时代最需要的是父亲的保护。

——西格蒙德·弗洛伊德

We only love truly once. It is the first time and succeeding passions are less uncontrolled.

——Du Coeur

真爱只有一次,就是初恋,之后的感情就不那么容易失控了。

——杜·克尔

Love is always present; it is just a matter of feeling it or not.

——Kimberly Kirberger

爱无时不有,无处不在,问题在于你能否感觉到。

——金伯利·基贝格尔

We always come back to our first love.

——Etienne

我们总是怀念初恋。

——艾蒂安

True love does not come by finding the perfect person, but by learning to see an imperfect person perfectly.

——Jason Jordan

获得真爱不是靠寻觅完美之人,而是学会把不完美之人看得完美。

——杰森·乔丹

Love sought is good, but given unsought is better.

——William Shakespeare

追求得到的爱情固然美好,但不经追求而得到的爱情更为美好。

——威廉·莎士比亚

Love is the triumph of imagination over intelligence.

——H. L. Mencken

爱情是想象战胜理智的硕果。

——H·L·门肯

A life without love in it is like a heap of ashes upon a deserted hearth, with the fire dead, the laughter stilled and the light extinguished.

——Frank Tebbets

生活没有爱如同被遗弃的炉灶里的一堆灰。火灭了，漆黑一片，再也没有了欢笑。

——弗兰克·特贝茨

Love and magic have a great deal in common. They enrich the soul, delight the heart. And they both take practice.

——Nora Roberts

爱情和魔术有许多共同之处：两者都能充实心灵，愉悦内心，而且都需要练习。

——诺拉·罗伯茨

In dreams and in love there are no impossibilities.

——Janos Arnay

在梦想和爱情里，一切皆有可能。

——雅诺什·阿内

Never let a problem to be solved become more important than a person to be loved.

——Barbara Johnson

决不让悬而未决的问题阻挡我们去爱应爱之人。

——巴巴拉·约翰逊

Love does not begin and end the way we seem to think it does. Love is a battle, love is a war; love is a growing up.

——James Baldwin

爱不会像我们设想的那样开始或结束。爱是战斗，爱是战争,爱是成长。

——詹姆斯·鲍德温

Men always want to be a woman's first love—women like to be a man's last romance.

——Oscar Wilde

男人总想做女人的初恋情人,女人想做男人的最后一个浪漫情侣。

——奥斯卡·王尔德

Love, while you are able to love.

——A. Frieligrath

趁着能爱,尽快去爱。

——A·弗里雷格拉夫

To fear love is to fear life, and those who fear life are already three parts dead.

——Bertrand Russell

害怕爱即害怕生活,害怕生活的人早已死了三分。

——伯特兰·罗素

We define love as a delight in the presence of the other person and an affirming of his value and development as much as one's own.

我们把爱情定义为与另一个人相处时的愉悦,是对对方的价值和发展的认同。

Once you have learned to love, you will have learned to live.

学会了爱也就学会了生活。

Love is the wisdom of the fool and the folly of the wise.

——Samuel Johnson

爱情体现愚者的智慧和智者的愚蠢。

——塞缪尔·约翰逊

The quickest way to receive love is to give; the fastest

way to lose love is to hold it too tightly; and the best way to keep love is to give it wings.

——Charles Caleb Colton

得到爱最快的方法就是付出；失去爱最快的方法就是紧抓；要想爱持久，就要给它翅膀。

——查尔斯·凯莱布·科尔顿

The secret of love is seeking variety in your life together, and never letting routine chords dull the melody of your romance.

爱情的秘诀就是让天天相守的时光充满变化，决不让一成不变的琴弦减弱浪漫的旋律。

There is no remedy for love but to love more.

——Henry David Thoreau

爱情没有解药，只有爱得更深。

——亨利·大卫·梭罗

Love is the great miracle cure. Loving ourselves works miracles in our lives.

爱是灵丹妙药。爱自己会在生活中创造奇迹。

Love may be blind, but it can sure find its way around in the dark!

爱情也许是盲目的,但是在黑暗中它会找到路。

Love is not finding someone to live with. It's finding someone you can't live without.

——Rafael Ortiz

爱情不是找个人一块生活,而是寻找那个生活中离不开的人。

——拉菲尔·奥尔蒂斯

Happiness lies in the secret heart of a lover.

幸福藏在情人的心中。

It is possible to learn more of a human being in one minute of love than in months of observation.

——Roman Rolland

要了解一个人,相恋一分钟可能胜过观察几个月。

——罗曼·罗兰

Love will enter cloaked in friendship's name.

——Ovid

爱情会打着友情的幌子闯入你的生活。

——奥维德

Let the first impulse pass, wait for the second.

——Baltasar Gracian

不要理会第一次的感情冲动，等待第二次吧。

——巴尔塔沙·格拉西安

First love is only a little foolishness and a lot of curiosity.

——George Bernard Shaw

初恋源于一点愚蠢和很多好奇。

——乔治·萧伯纳

First love is unforgettable all one's life.

——Maxim Gorky

初恋永生难忘。

——马克西姆·高尔基

They do not love that do not show their love.

——William Shakespeare

不表白爱便没有爱。

——威廉·莎士比亚

Love the heart that hurts you, but never hurt the heart that loves you.

——Vipin Sharma

爱伤你之心，勿伤爱你之心。

——维平·沙马

Love ceases to be a pleasure when it ceases to be a secret.

——Aphra Behn

爱情一旦公开，就失去了乐趣。

——阿夫拉·贝恩

Love is patient and kind; love is not jealous or boastful; it is not arrogant or rude.

爱是耐心和善良；爱不是忌妒和吹嘘；爱不是傲慢和粗鲁。

I believe love produces a certain flowering of the whole personality which nothing else can achieve.

——Ivan Sergeevich

我相信，只有爱情才能使人格发展成熟。

——伊万·谢尔盖耶维奇

A beautiful form is better than a beautiful face; a beautiful behavior than a beautiful form.

——Ralph Waldo Emerson

脸蛋美不如外形美,外形美不如行为美。

——拉尔夫·瓦尔多·爱默生

There is no greater invitation to love than loving first.

——St. Augustine

要想别人爱,首先爱别人。

——圣奥古斯丁

Love builds bridges where there are none.

——R. H. Delaney

爱在没桥之处搭建起一座座桥。

——R·H·德莱尼

I like not only to be loved, but to be told that I am loved.

——George Elliot

我不仅喜爱别人爱我,而且也喜欢有人对我说他爱我。

——乔治·艾略特

Love conquers all things; let us too surrender to Love.

——Virgil

爱情征服一切；让我们也向爱情屈服吧。

——维吉尔

Love is like pi—natural, irrational, and very important.

——Lisa Hoffman

爱就像圆周率——自然而然,不可理喻,至关重要。

——丽萨·霍夫曼

Love is like an hour glass, with the heart filling up as the brain empties.

——Jules Renord

爱就像沙漏,心装满了,头就空了。

——朱尔斯·雷诺德

Love is the difficult realization that something other than oneself is real.

——Murdoch

爱情让你终于认识到除了自身之外还有件事是那样真切。

——默多克

We are, each of us angels with only one wing; and we can only fly by embracing one another.

——Luciano de Crescenzo

我们人人都是独翼天使，只有相拥才能飞翔。

——卢西亚诺·德·克雷申佐

Love is not something you feel. It's something you do.

——David Wilkerson

爱不是感觉，而是行动。

——大卫·威尔克森

The hunger for love is much more difficult to remove than the hunger for bread.

——Mother Teresa

对爱的渴望要比对面包的渴望更难消除。

——特蕾莎修女

One word frees us of all the weight and pain of life. That word is love.

——Sophocles

一个字使我们摆脱了生活的沉重与痛苦，这个字就是爱。

——索福克勒斯

Those who love deeply never grow old; they may die of old age, but they die young.

——Arthur Wing Pinero

深深相爱的人永不会老去；他们可能因年龄而寿终,但他们离世时却依然年轻。

——亚瑟·温·皮内罗

Absence sharpens love, presence strengthens it.

分离爱更切,相聚爱弥坚。

Absence — that common cure of love.

——Judy Garland

别离——爱情的灵丹妙药。

——朱迪·加兰

In love the paradox occurs that two beings become one and yet remain two.

爱情的悖论是两个人合为一体,又各自独立。

A life without love is a sinful and immoral thing.

——Vincent van Gogh

没有爱的生活是罪恶的,不道德的。

——文森特·梵高

Love is a sweet torment.

爱情是一种甜蜜的折磨。

Love is a sweet tyranny, because the lover endures his torment willingly.

爱情是甜蜜的暴君,爱人心甘情愿地受他的折磨。

The pleasure of love is in loving.

——Duc De La Rochefoucauld

爱情的快乐在于去爱。

——拉罗什富科公爵

Love makes the wildest spirit tame, and the tamest spirit wild.

——Alexis Delp

再狂野的心,爱情也使之驯服;再驯服的心,爱情也使之狂野。

——亚历克西斯·德尔普

Love is the master key which opens the gates of happiness.

——Oliver Wendell Holmes

爱是打开幸福之门的万能钥匙。

——奥利弗·温德尔·霍姆斯

Life without love is like a tree without blossoms or fruit.

——Kahlil Gibran

没有爱情的生活就像既不开花也不结果的树。

——卡里·吉布兰

To love and be loved is to feel the sun from both sides.

——David Viscott

爱与被爱就像前身后背都能感受到太阳的温暖。

——大卫·维斯科特

Love is not just looking at each other, it's looking in the same direction.

——Antoine de Saint Exupéry

爱情不只是对视,而是朝同一方向看。

——安东尼·德·圣埃克苏佩里

In the arithmetic of love, one plus one equals everything, and two minus one equals nothing.

——Mignon Mclaughlin

在爱情的算术中，一加一等于一切，二减一等于零。

——米格恩·麦克劳克林

True love doesn't have a happy ending, because true love never ends.

真正的爱情没有幸福的结局，因为真正的爱情从不会结束。

Love must be as much a light, as it is a flame.

——Henry David Thoreau

爱情必须既是一盏灯，也是一团火。

——亨利·大卫·梭罗

Kissing is a means of getting two people so close together that they can't see anything wrong with each other.

——Rene Yasenek

亲吻使两个人如此贴近，看不到对方的任何缺点。

——雷尼·亚瑟内克

We were two and had but one heart between us.

——Francois Villon

我们是两个人却共有一颗心。

——弗朗索瓦·维庸

The reduction of the universe to a single being, the expansion of a single being even to God, this is love.

——Victor Hugo

把宇宙浓缩成一个人,把一个人想象成上帝——这就是爱。

——维克多·雨果

Love is a game that two can play and both win.

——Eva Gabor

爱情是一场两人参加并双赢的比赛。

——伊娃·加博尔

If you wish to be loved, love!

——Seneca

要想被爱,只有去爱!

——塞内加

You don’t love a woman because she’s beautiful; she is beautiful because you love her.

你不会因为女人美丽才爱她,而是因为爱她,她才美丽。

Life is a flower of which love is the honey.

——Victor Hugo

生活是鲜花,爱是花的蜜。

——维克多·雨果

Who loves, raves.

——Byron

恋爱者疯狂。

——拜伦

Every man is a poet when he is in love.

——Plato

每个恋爱中的人都是诗人。

——柏拉图

Where there is great love there are always miracles.

——Willa Cather

哪里有伟大的爱,哪里就会有奇迹。

——薇拉·凯瑟

Love is blind, and lovers cannot see the pretty follies that themselves commit.

——William Shakespeare

爱情是盲目的,恋人看不到自己所做的那些可爱的傻事。

——威廉·莎士比亚

You call it Madness, but I call it Love.

——Don Byas

你可以称它为疯狂,但我称之为爱情。

——唐·拜厄斯

True love comes quietly, without banners or flashing lights.

——Erich Segal

真爱悄悄光临,既不旗幡招展,也不灯火璀璨。

——埃里奇·塞加尔

Love is fire. But whether it's gonna warm your heart or burn your house down you can never tell.

——Jason Jordan

爱情是火,它要温暖你的心房还是要烧毁你的住房,你永远说不准。

——杰森·乔丹

For those passionately in love, the whole world seems to smile.

——David Myers

对那些热恋者而言，整个世界似乎都在微笑。

——大卫·迈尔思

You may conquer with the sword, but you are conquered by a kiss.

——Daniel Heinsius

你可以用剑征服别人，但是吻会征服你。

——丹尼尔·海因西厄斯

Love is friendship set on fire.

——Jeremy Irons

爱情是点燃的友谊。

——杰瑞米·艾恩思

We all suffer from the preoccupation that there exists, in the loved one, perfection.

——Sidney Poitier

我们都认为我们所爱的人是完美的。

——西德尼·普瓦蒂

There is no paradise on earth equal to the union of love and innocence.

——Jean Jacques Rousseau

人间最大的幸福莫如既有爱情又天真无邪。

——让·雅克·卢梭

Love is a little blind. When we love someone dearly, we unconsciously overlook many thoughts.

——Beatrice Saunders

爱情有一点盲目。深爱一个人时,我们下意识地忽略许多想法。

——比阿特丽斯·桑德斯

The essential sadness is to go through life without loving. But it would be almost equally sad to leave this world without ever telling those you loved that you love them.

——Krishna

没有爱的一生很可悲,而离开这个世界之前没有对你爱的人说你爱他,同样很可悲。

——克里希那

Take away love and our earth is a tomb.

——Robert Browning

没了爱,地球就是一座坟墓。

——罗伯特·勃朗宁

Love is life ... And if you miss love, you miss life.

——Leo Buscaglia

爱就是生活……你错过了爱,就是错过了生活。

——里昂·布斯卡格利亚

To be in love is merely to be in a perpetual state of anesthesia.

——H. L. Mencken

恋爱就是始终处于一种陶醉的状态。

——H·L·门肯

Gravitation can not be held responsible for people falling in love.

——Albert Einstein

地球引力与人坠入爱河无关。

——阿尔伯特·爱因斯坦

Wherever you are, I am there also.

——Ludwig van Beethoven

无论你走到哪里，我都与你形影不离。

——路德维希·范·贝多芬

Love has no price. It is only love if it is free.

——Melody Beattie

爱情是无价的。只有不标价的爱才是真爱。

——梅洛迪·贝蒂

To love is to receive a glimpse of heaven.

——Karen Sunde

爱就是受到上天的青睐。

——凯伦·森德

Put your hand on a hot stove for a minute, and it seems like an hour. Sit with a pretty girl for an hour, and it seems like a minute. That's relativity.

——Albert Einstein

把手在火炉上放一分钟，漫长得仿佛是一小时；跟美女一起坐一小时，短暂得像一分钟。这就是相对论。

——阿尔伯特·爱因斯坦

With love and patience, nothing is impossible.

——Daisaku Ikeda

有爱与耐心，一切皆有可能。

——大作 · 艾克达

I love you with all my heart. Thank you for being a special part of my life.

我用心爱着你，感谢你成为我生命中特殊的一部分。

Love reckons hours for months, and days for years; and every little absence is an age.

——John Dryden

一日不见如三秋，每次小别如隔世。

——约翰 · 德莱顿

Love from one being to another can only be that two solitudes come nearer, recognize and protect and comfort each other.

—— Han Suyin

相爱只能是两个人相近，相识，相护，相慰。

——韩素音

Those who have courage to love should have courage to suffer.

——Anthony Trollope

有勇气去爱就应有勇气去面对痛苦。

——安东尼·特罗洛普

Love is not blind—it sees more, not less. But because it sees more, it is willing to see less.

——Rabbi J. Gordon

爱情不是盲目的——它看到的更多,而不是更少。正因为看到的多,它才宁愿看的少。

——拉比·J·戈登

Never frown, even when you are sad, because you never know who is falling in love with your smile.

纵然伤心,也不要愁眉不展,因为说不准谁在爱你的微笑。

Respect is a form of love.

尊重是一种爱的表现。

Love that we can not have is the one that lasts the longest, hurts the deepest and feels the strongest.

不能拥有的爱持续最久,感受最强烈,伤害也最深。

We can never really love anybody with whom we never laugh.

——William Sloan Coffin

如果跟一个人在一起从未有过欢乐，你就不会真正爱上他。

——威廉·斯隆·科芬

Love is the flower you've got to let grow.

——John Lennon

爱情是株花，你要等它开放。

——约翰·列侬

Talk not of wasted affection; affection never was wasted.

——Henry Wadsworth Longfellow

不要说浪费了感情，感情从不会浪费。

——亨利·沃兹沃斯·朗费罗

Though you may travel the world to find the beautiful, you must have it within you or you will find it not.

——Ralph Waldo Emerson

周游世界去发现美，但心里必须有美，否则就发现不了。

——拉尔夫·瓦尔多·爱默生

Kindness, love, and consideration are not intrinsic to a child; they must be taught, along with everything else.

善良、爱和体贴并非孩子的本能，需要与其他事情一起教给孩子。

Pure love is a willingness to give without a thought of receiving anything in return.

纯洁的爱就是自愿奉献，不求回报。

Sorrow and trouble either soften the heart or harden it.

——James Mackintosh

悲哀和烦恼不是使人心软，就是使人心硬。

——詹姆士·麦金托什

The chance to love and be loved exists no matter where you are.

爱与被爱，随处都在。

Darkness cannot drive out darkness; only light can do that. Hate cannot drive out hate; only love can do that.

——Martin Luther King

黑暗不能驱赶黑暗，只有光明能够做到。仇恨不能赶走仇恨，只有爱能够做到。

——马丁·路德·金

The course of true love never did run smooth.

——William Shakespeare

真爱无坦途。

——威廉·莎士比亚

The only love worthy of a name is unconditional.

——John Powell

名副其实的爱就是无条件的爱。

——约翰·鲍威尔

Don't cry because it is over, smile because it happened.

不要为结束而哭泣，要为你曾经拥有而微笑。

When we lose one we love, our bitterest tears are called forth by the memory of hours when we loved not enough.

——Maurice Maeterlinck

失去爱人后，我们会因想起付出的爱不够而痛哭流涕。

——莫里斯·马特林克

With love, you should go ahead and take the risk of getting hurt because love is an amazing feeling.

——Britney Spears

爱情也许会使你受到伤害，但是你应该去爱，因为爱情是一种神奇的感觉。

——布兰妮・斯皮尔斯

Love is the child of illusion and the parent of disillusion.

——Sandy Wilson

幻想产生爱情，爱情导致幻灭。

——桑迪・威尔逊

Love is a tyrant sparing none.

——Pierre Corneille

爱情是人人都不放过的暴君。

——皮埃尔・高乃依

Tears may be dried up, but the heart—never.

——Marguerite de Valois

眼泪也许会干涸，但心永远不会枯竭。

——玛格丽特・德・瓦卢瓦

The pain of love is the pain of being alive. It is a perpetual wound.

——Maureen Duffy

爱的痛苦是有生之年的痛苦,是永恒的伤痛。

——莫林·达菲

If you have it [love], you don't need to have anything else. If you don't have it, it doesn't matter much what else you have.

——Sir James M. Barrie

如果你拥有爱情,你便别无它需。如果你没有爱情,你拥有的一切都无关紧要。

——詹姆斯·巴里爵士

It's better to have loved and lost than never to have lost at all.

——Samuel Butler

爱过又失去,胜似从未失去过。

——塞缪尔·巴特勒

Falling in love consists merely in uncorking the imagination and bottling the common sense.

——Helen Rowland

坠入爱河只不过是把想象力从瓶子中释放出来，把常识装进去。

——海伦·罗兰

One makes mistakes; that is life. But it is never a mistake to have loved.

——Romain Rolland

人人都犯错误，这就是生活，但是曾经爱过却绝非过错。

——罗曼·罗兰

Falling out of love is very enlightening. For a short while you see the world with new eyes.

——Iris Murdoch

失恋使人开悟。在一段时间内你就会用新的眼光看世界。

——艾瑞斯·默多克

Love is a choice you make from moment to moment.

——Barbara de Angelis

爱情是时时要做的选择。

——巴巴拉·德·安杰利斯

You don't know who is important to you until you actually lose them.

——Mahatma Gandhi

只有真正失去了,你才懂得谁对你是重要的。

——圣雄甘地

Had we not loved ourselves at all, we could never have been obliged to love anything. So that self love is the basis of all love.

——Thomas Traherne

假如我们从未爱过自己,就不可能爱过任何东西。爱自己是一切爱的基础。

——托马斯·特拉赫姆

To say the truth, reason and love keep little company together nowadays.

——William Shakespeare

说真话,现在理智和爱情水火难相容。

——威廉·莎士比亚

We can only learn to love by loving.

——Iris Murdoch

我们只有通过爱去学会爱。

———艾瑞斯·默多克

The sweetest joy, the wildest woe is love.

——Pearl Bailey

最甜蜜的快乐、最钻心的痛苦，就是爱情。

——珀尔·贝利

I am happy, because I love, because I have love.

—— Browning

我是幸福的，因为我爱，因为我有爱。

——勃朗宁

You can't buy love, but you can pay heavily for it.

——Henny Youngman

你买不到爱情，但你可以为之付出高昂的代价。

——亨利·扬曼

Love is shown in your deeds, not in your words.

——Jerome Cummings

爱见于行而不见于言。

——杰罗姆·卡明斯

Pure love and suspicion cannot dwell together: at the door where the latter enters, the former makes its exit.

——Alexandre Dumas

纯洁的爱情和无端的猜疑水火不容：起了疑心，丢了爱情。

——亚历山大·仲马

There are three things men can do with women: love them, suffer for them, or turn them into literature.

——Stephen Stills

对于女人，男人可以做三件事：爱她们，为她们受苦，或者把她们写进文学。

——史蒂芬·施蒂尔斯

Love lasts as long as the memory endures.

——William Caxton

记忆不灭，爱情永存。

——威廉·卡克斯顿

The great tragedy of life is not that men perish, but that they cease to love.

——W. Somerset Maugham

人生的悲剧不在于死亡，而在于停止去爱。

——W·萨默塞特·毛姆

The art of love is largely the art of persistence.

——Albert Ellis

爱的艺术在很大程度上就是坚持不懈的艺术。

——阿尔伯特·埃利斯

The only abnormality is the incapacity to love.

——Anais Nin

唯一的反常就是欠缺爱的能力。

——阿奈丝·尼恩

All love that has not friendship for its base, is like a mansion built upon sand.

——Ella Wheeler Wilcox

没有友情基础的爱情犹如建在沙地上的大厦。

——埃拉·惠勒·威尔科克斯

What a grand thing, to be loved! What a grander thing still, to love!

——Victor Hugo

有人爱,多么美好！爱别人,更美好！

——维克多·雨果

To love and win is the best thing. To love and lose, the next best.

——William M. Thackeray

爱会成功最好，爱遇挫折次之。

——威廉 · M · 萨克雷

Faults are thick where love is thin.

——Dicky Fox

一朝情意淡，样样不顺眼。

——迪克 · 福克斯

Of all pains, the greatest pain is to love, and love in vain.

——George Granville

苦中之苦，莫过于爱而无果。

——乔治 · 格兰维尔

If our love is only a will to possess, it is not love.

如果我们的爱仅仅是占有欲，那就不是爱。

Marriage has many pains, but celibacy has no pleasures.

——Samuel Johnson

婚姻虽苦多，独身没乐趣。

——塞缪尔 · 约翰逊

The greatest thing in the world is to be in love and be loved in return.

世界上最伟大的事情就是爱与被爱。

Marriage is the grave or tomb of wit.

——Margaret Cavendish

婚姻是智慧的坟墓。

——玛格丽特·卡文迪什

The love we give away is the only love we keep.

——Elbert Hubbard

付出的爱是唯一拥有的爱。

——艾尔伯特·哈伯德

Age does not protect you from love but love to some extent protects you from age.

——Jeanne Moreau

年龄不影响爱情,但爱情在某种程度上使人年轻。

——珍妮·莫罗

If you would marry suitably, marry your equal.

——Ovid

要想婚姻称心如意，双方必须相匹配。

——奥维德

It's a truth universally acknowledged, that a single man in possession of a good fortune must be in want of a wife.

——Jane Austin

凡是有钱人都要娶一个太太，这是一条举世公认的真理。

——简・奥斯丁

You can give without loving, but you cannot love without giving.

——Amy Carmichael

可以付出而不去爱，但却不可以去爱而不付出。

——艾米・卡迈克尔

Marriage is a bribe to make a house keeper think she's a householder.

——Thornton Wilder

婚姻就是贿赂家庭主妇，让她觉得她是一家之主。

——桑顿・怀尔德

A successful marriage requires falling in love many times, always with the same person.

——Mignon Mclaughlin

美满的婚姻需要相爱多次,但爱的总是同一个人。

——米格恩·麦克劳克林

Keep your eyes open before marriage, and half shut afterwards.

——Benjamin Franklin

婚前睁大眼,婚后半闭眼。

——本杰明·富兰克林

My wife heard me say "I love you" a thousand times, but she never once heard me say sorry.

——Bruce Willis

我妻子听到我说"我爱你" 1000 次,但从没听我说过一句"对不起"。

——布鲁斯·威尔斯

It is impossible to love and be wise.

——Bacon

恋爱、理智难共存。

——培根

Man's best possession is a sympathetic wife.

——Euripides

男人最好的财产是有一位情投意合的妻子。

——欧里庇得斯

Love is like a violin. The music may stop now and then, but the strings remain forever.

——June Masters Bacher

爱好比小提琴。音乐可以时停时起,而琴弦伴琴,永不分离。

——琼·马斯特斯·巴彻

Love is an ideal thing, marriage a real thing; a confusion of the real with the ideal never goes unpunished.

——Goethe

爱情是理想化的,婚姻是现实的。把二者混为一谈就要遭殃。

——歌德

A good marriage is one which allows for change and growth in the individuals and in the way they express their love.

——Pearl Buck

美满婚姻能让人改变并成长，表达爱的方式也会随之变化加强。

——赛珍珠

Love is but the discovery of ourselves in others, and the delight in the recognition.

——Alexander Smith

爱就是在别人身上找到我们自己，就是这种自我发现带来的喜悦。

——亚历山大·史密斯

Love is a part of man's life; it is a woman's whole existence.

爱是男人生活的一部分，它却是女人生活的全部。

A good husband makes a good wife.

——Robert Burton

好丈夫造就好妻子。

——罗伯特·伯顿

A man falls in love through his eyes, a woman through her ears.

——Woodrow Wyatt

男人通过眼睛去爱，女人通过耳朵去爱。

——伍德罗·怀亚特

A successful marriage is an edifice that must be rebuilt every day.

——Andre Maurois

成功的婚姻是座天天都要重建的大厦。

——安德烈·莫罗阿

The best proof of love is trust.

——Joyce Brothers

爱的最好证明是信任。

——乔伊斯·布拉泽斯

Better is a dinner of herbs where love is, than a stalled ox and hatred there with.

——Charlotte Bronte

相亲相爱吃糠咽菜胜似有仇有恨大酒大肉。

——夏洛特·勃朗特

To love is to place our happiness in the happiness of another.

——G. W.von Leibnitz

爱就是把我们的幸福融入另一个人的幸福之中。

——G·W·凡·莱布尼茨

Intimacy is what makes a marriage, not a ceremony, not a piece of paper from the state.

——Kathleen Norris

婚姻的真谛既不是仪式也不是国家的一纸证书，而是亲密无间的感情。

——凯瑟琳·诺里斯

Great loves too must be endured.

——Coco Chanel

伟大的爱情也必须忍耐。

——可可·香奈儿

People who are sensible about love are incapable of it.

——Douglas Yates

谁在爱情上讲究理智，谁就没有能力去爱。

——道格拉斯·耶茨

It is best to love wisely, no doubt; but to love foolishly is better than not to be able to love at all.

——William Makepeace Thackeray

当然爱得明智再好不过，但即使爱得愚蠢也胜过一点都不能爱。

——威廉·梅克比斯·萨克雷

Love is love's reward.

——John Dryden

付出爱，收获爱。

——约翰·德莱顿

And in the end, the love we take will be equal to the love we make.

最终，我们得到的爱会等于我们付出的爱。

Heirlooms we don't have in our family. But stories we've got.

——Rose Cherin

尽管家里没有传家宝，我们却有自己的故事。

——罗斯·切林

Call it a clan, call it a network, call it a tribe, call it a family. Whatever you call it, whoever you are, you need one.

——Jane Howard

不管你是谁，不管你如何称呼它，人人都需要一个——无论你称之为氏族、网络，还是部落、家庭。

——简·霍华德

Happiness is having a large, loving, caring, close-knit family in another city.

——George Burns

幸福就是在另外一个城市里拥有一个充满了爱与关心、和睦亲密的大家庭。

——乔治·彭斯

Whom we love best to them we can say least.

对我们最爱的人，我们可以说得最少。

A happy family is but an earlier heaven.

——John Bowring

幸福的家庭就是人间天堂。

——约翰·鲍林

The only rock I know that stays steady, the only institution I know that works, is the family.

——Lee Iacocca

我所知道的唯一稳固的基石、唯一发挥作用的组织，就是家庭。

——李·艾科卡

All happy families resemble one another, each unhappy family is unhappy in its own way.

——Leo Tolstoy

幸福的家庭都是相似的，不幸的家庭各有各的不幸。

——列夫·托尔斯泰

A house divided against itself cannot stand.

家有内讧难维系。

East or west, home is best.

东也好，西也好，还是家最好。

Every bird likes its own nest the best.

金窝银窝，不如自己的草窝。

Family isn't about whose blood you have. It's about who you care about.

——Trey Parker & Matt Stone

家的意义不在于你体内流的是谁的血，而在于你关心的是谁。

——特力·帕克、迈特·斯通

The bond that links your true family is not one of blood, but of respect and joy in each other's life.

——Richard Bach

真正联结家庭的纽带不是血缘，而是带给彼此生活的喜悦和尊重。

——理查德·巴赫

Friendship lasts a day, kinship lasts forever.

友谊维系一天，亲情相伴一生。

Home is where the heart is.

家是心之所系。

Family faces are magic mirrors. Looking at people who belong to us, we see the past, present and future.

——Gail Lumet Buckley

家人的脸是神奇的魔镜。看着他们，我们就看到了过去、现在和未来。

——盖尔·卢米特·巴克利

A healthy family is sacred territory.

健康的家庭是圣地。

The happiest moments of my life have been the few which I have passed at home in the bosom of my family.

——Thomas Jefferson

我生命中最幸福的短暂时光是在家人的怀抱中度过的。

——托马斯·杰斐逊

There is no place like home.

再好的地方也不如家。

Smile at each other, make time for each other in your family.

多对家人微笑,多给家人一点时间。

It is indeed a desirable thing to be well descended, but the glory belongs to our ancestors.

——Plutarch

有好的家世固然令人羡慕,但是光荣属于祖先。

——普卢塔克

Kinship is healing; we are physicians to each other.

骨肉亲情是抚慰疾苦的良药。

Sooner or later we all quote our mothers.

——Bern Williams

迟早我们都会引述母亲的话。

——伯恩·威廉姆斯

A mother is not a person to lean on but a person to make leaning unnecessary.

——Dorothy C. Fisher

母亲不是孩子依赖的人,而是培养孩子无须依赖的人。

——多罗西·C·费希尔

The most important thing she'd learned over the years was that there was no way to be a perfect mother and a million ways to be a good one.

——Jill Churchill

多年来她明白的最重要的事情是:要当完美母亲不可能,做好母亲的方法成千上万。

——吉尔·丘吉尔

My mother had a great deal of trouble with me, but I think she enjoyed it.

——Mark Twain

我给母亲带来不少麻烦,但我觉得她乐在其中。

——马克·吐温

How many hopes and fears, how many ardent wishes and anxious apprehensions are twisted together in the threads that connect the parents with the child!

——Samuel G. Goodrich

无数的希望和担忧,无数的祝福和理解,如交织的丝线将父母和孩子紧紧连在一起。

——塞缪尔·G·吉德里奇

A mother's love never changes.

母爱永恒。

For a mother the project of raising a boy is the most fulfilling project she can hope for.

——Andrea Dworkin

母亲所能期待的最有成就感的事业就是养育一个孩子。

——安德里亚·德沃金

It is a wise father that knows his own child.

——William Shakespeare

再聪明的父亲也未必了解自己的孩子。

——威廉·莎士比亚

From the father comes honour; from the mother, comfort.

荣誉由父赐,安慰由母给。

Before I got married, I had six theories about bringing up children. Now I have six children and no theories.

——John Wilmot

结婚之前我有六套培养孩子的理论；现在我有六个孩子却没有任何理论。

——约翰·华尔莫特

The joys of parents are secret, and so are their grieves and fears.

——Francis Bacon

父母的喜悦、悲痛和畏惧都隐藏于内心。

——弗朗西斯·培根

Being a grownup means assuming responsibility for

yourself, for your children, and—here's the big curve—for your parents.

——Wendy Wasserstein

成年意味着对自己、对孩子负责；此外，还要回过头来对父母负责。

——温迪·瓦瑟斯坦

Some are kissing mothers and some are scolding mothers, but it is love just the same, and most mothers kiss and scold together.

——Pearl S. Buck

有的母亲慈爱，有的母亲严厉，而母爱是相同的，大多数母亲既慈爱又严厉。

——赛珍珠

It is the general rule, that all superior men inherit the elements of superiority from their mother.

一个普遍规律：所有优秀的人通常都从母亲那里继承优秀的品质。

Judicious mothers will always keep in mind, that they

are the first book read, and the last put aside, in every child's library.

——C. Lenox Redmond

明智的母亲会谨记：她们是每个孩子自己的图书馆中读到的第一本书，也是最后放下的那本书。

——C·鲁诺·雷蒙德

The art of mothering is to teach the art of living to children.

——Elaine Heffner

做母亲的艺术就是教会孩子生活的艺术。

——伊莱恩·海弗纳

Like mother, like daughter.

有其母必有其女。

Mothers are fonder than fathers of their children because they are more certain they are their own.

——Aristotle

母亲较之父亲更喜爱孩子，因为她们更肯定孩子是自己的。

——亚里士多德

Don't hold your parents up to contempt. After all, you are their son, and it is just possible that you may take after them.

不要瞧不起父母。毕竟你是他们的孩子,很有可能你会像他们。

One good mother is worth a hundred schoolmasters.

一位好母亲顶得上一百个教师。

To understand your parents' love, you must raise children yourself.

不养儿不知父母恩。

The ideal mother, like the ideal marriage, is a fiction.

——Milton R. Sapirstein

完美的母亲如同完美的婚姻一样可遇不可求。

——米尔顿·R·萨丕尔斯坦

Every generation revolts against its fathers and makes friends with its grandfathers.

——Lewis Mumford

每一代人都反抗父亲,却与祖父为友。

——路易斯·芒福德

Children are the parents's riches.

子女是父母的财富。

Children begin by loving their parents; as they grow older they judge them; sometimes they forgive them.

——Oscar Wilde

孩子起先热爱父母；长大后他们评价父母，有时宽恕父母。

——奥斯卡·王尔德

Blood is thicker than water.

血浓于水。

The most important thing that parents can teach their children is how to get along without them.

——Frank A. Clark

父母能教给孩子的最重要的事情是如何独立生活。

——弗兰克·A·克拉克

Like begets like./Like cow, like calf./Like father, like son.

有其父必有其子。

One father is more than a hundred schoolmasters.

——George Herbert

一个父亲胜似一百个教师。

——乔治·赫伯特

All I am, or can be, I owe to my angel mother.

——Abraham Lincoln

我的成就、我的能力,都归功于我慈祥的母亲。

——亚伯拉罕·林肯

We never know the love of the parents until we become parents ourselves.

——Henry Ward Beecher

直到我们自己成了父母才明白父母之爱。

——亨利·沃德·比彻

There is no friendship, no love, like that of the parent for the child.

——Henry Ward Beecher

友情、爱情不如舐犊之情。

——亨利·沃德·比彻

Families with babies and families without babies are sorry for each other.

有孩子和没孩子的家庭彼此同情。

Don’t be discouraged if your children reject your advice. Years later they will offer it to their own offspring.

不要因孩子拒绝你的建议而沮丧；多年以后他们会给自己的孩子同样的建议。

Where children are, there is the golden age.

——Novalis

拥有孩子的岁月是美好的时光。

——诺瓦利斯

Kids used to ask where they came from, now they tell you where to go.

过去孩子常常问他们从哪里来，现在则告诉你他们要到哪里去。

Happy is he that is happy in his children.

对自己孩子感到高兴的，才是幸福的人。

Many children, many cares; no children, no felicity.

——Christian Nevell Bovee

孩子多,心事多; 但是没有孩子,就没有幸福。

——克里斯汀 · 内维尔 · 波弗

My son is my son, till he hath got him a wife; but my daughter's my daughter all the days of her life.

儿子只有在娶妻前是儿子,女儿则终生是女儿。

Human beings are the only creatures that allow their children to come back home.

——Bill Cosby

人类是唯一允许孩子回家的生物。

——比尔 · 科斯比

Be gentle with the young.

——Juvenal

对孩子要温柔。

——尤维纳尔

Life affords no greater responsibility, no greater privilege, than the raising of the next generation.

——C. Everett Koop

抚养下一代是生活赋予我们最大的责任和特权。

——C·艾弗莱特·库普

Lucky that man whose children make his happiness in life and not his grief, the anguished disappointment of his hopes.

——Euripides

孩子给一个人的生活带来快乐,而非忧伤和希望破灭的痛苦,那么这个人就是幸运的。

——欧里庇得斯

I have found the best way to give advice to your children is to find out what they want and then advise them to do it.

——Harry S. Truman

给孩子提供建议最好的办法就是弄清楚他们想要什么,然后建议他们付诸行动。

——哈利·S·杜鲁门

Good children make glad parents.

孩子好,父母笑。

He that has no children knows not what is love.

没有孩子的人,不懂什么叫爱。

If you can give your son or daughter only one gift, let it be enthusiasm.

——Bruce Barton

如果你只能给你的孩子一件礼物,那么给他们热情吧。

——布鲁斯·巴顿

Children are our most valuable natural resources.

——Herbert Clark Hoover

孩子是我们最宝贵的自然资源。

——赫伯特·克拉克·胡佛

Children are the keys to paradise.

——Richard Henry Stoddard

孩子是打开天堂大门的钥匙。

——理查德·亨利·斯托达德

You know that children are growing up when they start asking questions that have answers.

——John J. Plomp

当孩子开始提出有答案的问题时,他们就长大了。

——约翰·J. 普洛姆朴

It is harder to marry a daughter well than to bring her up well.

养女容易嫁女难。

There was a time when we expected nothing of our children but obedience, as opposed to the present, when we expect everything of them but obedience.

——Anatole Broyard

我们曾对孩子除了要求顺从外别无所求；而今可以期待孩子其他事情，就是不能指望他们顺从。

——安纳托尔·卜若雅

A little child is the sweetest and purest thing in the world.

幼儿是世界上最可爱、最纯洁的。

Children are living jewels dropped unsustained from heaven.

——Robert Pollok

孩子是天上落下的珠宝。

——罗伯特·波勒克

So long as little children are allowed to suffer, there is no true love in this world.

——Isadora Duncan

如果叫小孩子受苦,世上便没有真正的爱。

——伊莎多拉·邓肯

Judicious praise is to children what the sun is to flowers.

——Bertrand Russell

明智的表扬对孩子们的作用,犹如阳光对于花朵的作用。

——伯特兰·罗素

Children have more need of models than critics.

——Joseph Joubert

孩子更需要的是榜样,而不是批评。

——约瑟夫·朱伯特

It was the policy of the good old gentlemen to make his children feel that home was the happiest place in the world.

——Washington Irving

古往贤者都会使孩子感到家庭是世界上最幸福的地方。

——华盛顿·欧文

A mother's happiness is like a beacon, lighting up the future but reflected also on the past in the guise of fond memories.

——Balzac

母亲的幸福如同火把,照亮孩子的前途,留给孩子美好的记忆。

——巴尔扎克

He is the happiest, be he King or peasant, who finds peace in his home.

——Goethe

无论是国王还农夫,家庭和睦是最幸福的。

——歌德

If you want your children to keep their feet on the ground, put some responsibility on their shoulders.

——John Bryant

若希望你的孩子脚踏实地,就让他们负些责任。

——约翰·布赖恩特

The sooner you treat your son as a man, the sooner he will be one.

越早把你的儿子当成男人,他就越早成为男人。

A placid parent makes a placid home.

平和的父母创造温馨的家。

A mother's voice is the most beautiful sound in the world.

母亲的呼唤是世上最美的声音。

From your parents you learn love and laughter and how to put one foot before the other.

你从父母那里学会爱,学会美,学会怎样走路。

Family is the harbor of love.

家是爱的港湾。

朋友与情谊

To have joy one must share it. Happiness was born a twin.

——Lord Byron

快乐须分享,分享才快乐。

——拜伦勋爵

When a friend is in trouble, don't annoy him by asking if there is anything you can do. Think up something appropriate and do it.

——Edgar Watson Howe

朋友有难,问他需要什么帮助只会烦扰他。想想该做什么合适,只管做。

——艾德加·沃森·豪

Remember, the greatest gift is not found in a store nor under a tree, but in the hearts of true friends.

记住,最重要的礼物不在商店里也不在圣诞树下,而在真正的朋友心中。

You shall judge a man by his foes as well as by his friends.

判断一个人的为人,可以通过他的朋友,也可以通过他的敌人。

Tell me who's your friend and I'll tell you who you are.

告诉我你的朋友，我就能告诉你的为人。

We should never remember the benefits we have offered, not forget the favor received.

做点好事别提起，别人恩情要牢记。

He who loses wealth loses much; he who loses a friend loses more; but he that loses his courage loses all.

失去财富的人失去了很多，失去朋友的人失去得更多，而失去勇气的人则失去了全部。

I do then with my friends as I do with my books. I would have them where I can find them, but I seldom use them.

——Ralph Waldo Emerson

我对待朋友就像对待书一样，把他们放在能够找到的地方，却很少用他们。

——拉尔夫·瓦尔多·爱默生

Do you know what friendship is? It is to be brother and sister; two souls which touch without mingling, two fingers on one hand.

——Victor Hugo

你知道友谊是什么吗？友谊就是要做兄弟姐妹；友谊是两个心灵相触却不合二为一，是一只手上的两个手指。

——维克多·雨果

Poverty is the test of civility and the touchstone of friendship.

贫穷是对人情的考验，也是友情的试金石。

Research shows that strong, supportive friendships help us to be healthier, as well as happier. In fact, some scientists have called friendship the vaccine, that protects both physical and mental health!

研究表明相互支持的牢固友谊使人更健康，更幸福。科学家称友谊为维护精神与身体健康的疫苗。

Friends are like rainbows; they come to brighten your life after a storm.

朋友如彩虹，风雨过后给你生活带来光明。

Some friends you have to make an effort to appreciate; others, you simply look forward to spending time with.

有些朋友需要费力欣赏，有些朋友就盼着与其共度时光。

Sensitive people are often shy. But that doesn't mean they can't find good friends, usually in a one-to-one situation rather than at social gatherings.

敏感的人常常害羞，这并不意味着他们找不到朋友，通常喜欢一对一交往，而不是在一起参加聚会。

Our old friends are trees that we have planted in the garden of love. Our new friends are flowers that bloom for a summer, and perhaps next year, too.

老朋友是我们种在爱的花园里的树，新朋友是夏天盛开的花朵，也许明年还能开。

Friends agree best at distance.

君子之交淡如水。

Friends are like fiddle-strings, they must not be screwed too tight.

琴弦勿拧太紧，朋友不可过亲。

Friends that desert us in the hour of need are friends in name, not in reality.

困难时背弃我们的朋友有名无实。

Fall sick and you will see who is your friend and who is not.

危难见友情。

A friend is easier lost than found.

失友容易交友难。

True friendship is never serene.

真正的友谊从来不是相安无事。

He gives twice who gives quickly.

及时的帮助相当于双倍的帮助。

Good advice is beyond price.

忠告乃无价之宝。

It is good to have friends in trouble.

困境得友是幸事。

No person is your friend who demands your silence, or denies your right to grow.

——Alice Walker

要求你沉默,或者否认你有权发展的人不是你的朋友。

——爱丽丝·沃克

Friendships are fragile things, and require as much handling as any other fragile and precious thing.

——Randolph S. Bourne

友谊是脆弱的,需要像对待其他易碎的珍贵物品一样加以呵护。

——伦道夫·S·伯恩

If we would build on a sure foundation in friendship, we must love friends for their sake rather than for our own.

——Charlotte Bronte

要想友情基础稳固,必须为朋友的缘故爱朋友,而非因为自己。

——夏洛特·勃朗特

Do not remove a fly from your friend's head with a hatchet.

不要用斧头赶走朋友头上的苍蝇。

In speaking well of others, you speak well of yourself.

赞美他人,也是在赞美自己。

The better you know someone, the less there is to say. Or maybe, there's less that needs to be said.

越了解某人,越无话可说,也许越无须多说。

He that speaks me fair and loves me not, I'll speak him fair and trust him not.

对只讲我好话不爱我的人,我也说他好话,而不信任他。

Be careful of what you say, friendship can end in one minute because of a stupid word.

留心自己说的话,友情可能因为一句愚蠢的话瞬间结束。

Friendship is constant in all other things, save in the office and affairs of love.

——William Shakespeare

办公室里和爱情里的友谊不如其他任何地方的友谊稳固。

——威廉·莎士比亚

False friendship, like the ivy, decays and ruins the walls it embraces; but true friendship gives new life and animation to the object it supports.

——Richard Burton

虚假的友谊就像常春藤，损坏其攀附的墙；而真正的友谊赋予其支撑物以新生命和活力。

——理查德·伯顿

Friends are lost by calling often and calling seldom.

交往过密过疏，都会失去朋友。

Diffidence is the poison of friendship.

疑心是友谊的毒药。

Trust not a new friend nor an old enemy.

不要相信新朋，也不要相信旧敌。

Better an intelligent enemy than an ignorant friend.

——Sadi

聪明的敌人胜过无知的朋友。

——萨迪

Better lose a jest than a friend.

宁可少说俏皮话，也不开罪朋友。

You will never have a perfect friendship, but you must strive for one.

你永远不会拥有完美的友情，但你必须奋力去争取。

Community of purpose makes friendship.

目标一致生友谊。

Kindnesses, like grain, increase by sowing.

友善犹如粮食，一分耕耘，一分收获。

Friendship is a plant which must be often watered.

友谊是树，需常浇灌。

Friendship lasts when each friend thinks he has a slight superiority over the other.

——Honore de Balzac

朋友之间互相都觉得比对方略胜一筹，友谊才能持续下去。

——奥诺雷·德·巴尔扎克

Two persons cannot long be friends if they cannot forgive each other's little failings.

——Jean de La Brugere

如果两人不能原谅彼此的小缺点,友谊便不会长久。

——让·德·拉·布吕耶尔

An irritable man is like a hedgehog rolled up the wrong way, tormenting himself with his own prickles.

——Thomas Hood

易怒的人像一只反过来蜷缩的刺猬,用自己的刺折磨自己。

——托马斯·胡德

A long walk in the countryside, in the company of a good friend, is one of life's greatest joys.

与挚友乡间游,人生乐悠悠。

Reach out to help a friend in need —you can help them to see light at the end of the tunnel.The journey is the reward.

朋友有难,出手相助。帮他们看到隧道尽头的光明,你也可以尽享助人之乐。

If you are quick to choose your friends, you may be quick to change them.

交朋友快,换朋友快。

Happiness is not all about you—it's about sharing with others.

幸福并非只关乎自己,而且还须分享。

Gratitude is good for us. It increases positive emotion and decreases the negative.

感恩之心利于身心,促人向上,避免消极。

A simple "hello" to a neighbour can make us feel happier and more secure about where we live.

与邻居简单打个招呼,心情更愉悦,心里更踏实。

Giving support and receiving it from others helps us to be happy.

相互支持,增进幸福。

Happiness held is the seed; happiness shared is the flower.

握在手中的幸福是种子,分享的幸福才是花朵。

Friendship has a stronger effect on happiness than income.

友谊比收入更影响幸福指数。

Do not speak of your happiness to one less fortunate than yourself.

——Plutarch

不要与不如你幸运的人谈论你的幸福。

——普鲁塔克

That friendship will not continue to the end that is begun for an end.

——Francis Quareles

别有用心的友情不会长久。

——弗朗西斯·夸瑞尔斯

The insolent have no friends.

傲慢无礼的人没有朋友。

A broken friendship may be soldered, but will never be sound.

破裂的友谊,再弥补也无法和好如初。

Lend your money, and lose your friend.
借出钱财,失去朋友。

A thankful person is thankful under all circumstances.
感恩的人任何情况下都会心存感念。

Better to be alone than in bad company.
交友宁缺毋滥。

Friendship increases in visiting friends, but in visiting them seldom.

——Thomas Fuller

要访友,勿勤访友,友情才会加深。

——托马斯·富勒

Be a friend to thyself, and others will be so, too.
做自己的朋友,别人也会做你的朋友。

Try your friend before you trust him.
朋友要经考验,才能取得信任。

Constant criticism is highly destructive in relationships. For every negative comment, find five positive ones to add.

批评不断，破坏关系；一次批评，须有五次鼓励。

Compliment someone whose behaviour has impressed you, even if you feel shy about doing so. Most people will appreciate it.

遇感人言行，要不吝赞美，莫羞于出口。溢美之词会令多数人心存感激。

Sharing our thoughts and needs makes us feel valued and understood.

交流思想，了解需求，相互尊重，相互理解。

All things being equal, people will do business with a friend; all things being unequal, people will still do business with a friend.

——Mark Mccormack

同等条件下，人们会和朋友做生意；不同等条件下，人们还是会和朋友做生意。

——马克·麦克考马克

If you see a friend without a smile, give him one of yours.

如果你看到一个不带微笑的朋友，给他微笑。

Many hands make light work.

人多易做事。

Victories and defeats are transient, while friendship is ever lasting.

胜负瞬间过，友谊却永存。

Nothing makes the earth seem so spacious as to have friends at a distance; they make the latitudes and longitudes.

——Henry David Thoreau

唯有远方有朋友，天地才显得如此宽广；有了朋友才有了纬度和经度。

——亨利·大卫·梭罗

Friendship that flows from the heart cannot be frozen by adversity, as the water that flows from the spring can not congeal in winter.

——James Fennimore Cooper

喷泉流出的水不会在冬季结冰；发自内心的友情也不会由于困境而冻结。

——詹姆士·菲尼摩尔·库珀

Friends are needed both for joy and for sorrow.

——Samuel Paterson

喜悦和痛苦时都需要朋友。

——塞缪尔·帕特森

Never trust a man who speaks well of everybody.

谁的好话都说的人,不可信。

A ready way to lose friend is to lend him money.

失友都因借钱起。

To find a friend one must close one eye. To keep him, two.

——Norman Douglas

觅一知己,需闭一只眼;守一知己,需闭两只眼。

——诺曼·道格拉斯

The greatest good you can do for another is not just to share your riches but to reveal to him his own.

——Benjamin Disraeli

给人最大的帮助,不单是让他分享你的财富,而且还向他指明他自己的富有。

——本杰明·迪斯雷利

The only service a friend can really render is to keep your courage by holding up to you a mirror in which you can see a noble image of yourself.

——George Bernard Shaw

朋友能确切提供的唯一服务就是举起一面镜子,让你看到自己的高贵形象,鼓足自己的勇气。

——乔治·萧伯纳

You realize you have made a friend when silence falls between you, and it doesn't make either of you feel uncomfortable.

如果两人之间不说话不觉得尴尬,你会意识到你交了一个朋友。

One of life's greatest pleasures is reminiscing about past times, good or bad, with an old and trusted friend. It helps us to know that there are others who remember our lives, have shared them with us, and continue to do so.

人生的最大乐趣就是与可靠的老朋友回忆过去的好时光或坏时光,让我们知道有人记着我们的生活,与我们分享并继续分享我们的生活。

A friend is someone you can be silly with, and never feel embarrassed for a moment.

在他面前出洋相，而丝毫不会感到尴尬，那这个人就是朋友。

A friend who is far away is sometimes much nearer than one who is at hand.

远方的朋友有时感觉近在咫尺，而有人近在咫尺却像远在天边。

When you prosper, you will find many friends; in times of adversity, most of them will disappear. The few who remain are the ones to cherish throughout your life.

发达之时，门庭若市，败落之时，门可罗雀，不离不弃者是终生珍视的朋友。

True friendship is not based on glamour or success. It arises spontaneously, between two people who take a liking to each other, for no reason other than that.

真正的友谊不是基于魅力或成功，而纯粹是两人之间情投意合，除此之外没有任何其他原因。

A good friend gives you courage to face life's challenges.

好朋友给你勇气以面对生活挑战。

The best preservative to keep the mind in health is the faithful admonition of a friend.

——Francis Bacon

朋友的忠告是保持心理健康的最好保健品。

——弗朗西斯·培根

Say " thank you" to your friend, often, and from the heart. However close you are to each other, nobody likes to be taken for granted.

常对朋友表示真心感谢。不管关系多么密切,没有人喜欢自己的付出被当作是理所当然的。

To have even one good friend in life is a blessing.

一生有一位好友就是福分。

Our friends help us to measure, and value, the stages we go through in life: the energy of childhood; the excitement of teenage years; the ambition of young adulthood; the maturity of middle age; and finally, the tranquillity of old age.

朋友让我们审视、评估人生的各个阶段：童年活泼好动，少年激情四射，青年雄心勃勃，中年老成持重，老年平心静气。

From time to time, you may have to tell your friend a few white lies. If that's the case, remember, being kind is sometimes more important than being brutally honest.

有时可能不得不对朋友撒个无害的谎，遇到这种情况，记住善良比说伤人的实话更重要。

There are few human beings in the world who do not wish, in their hearts, that they had many good friends.

世界上没有几个人会不希望自己有很多朋友的。

A true friend does not envy your success, or despise your failure.

真正的朋友不会嫉妒你的成功或蔑视你的失败。

The sweetness of a true friend's smile, their kiss of gratitude for a small favour or gift, is one of life's greatest joys.

挚友甜蜜的微笑、因为帮了小忙或礼物而获得感激的亲吻是人生最大的乐趣之一。

Don't be envious of a popular, successful person who appears to have many friends; when times get hard, he or she may not find one true friend among them.

不要妒羡受欢迎的成功人物。他好像有很多朋友，一旦有难也许一个真正的朋友也没有。

Behave with consideration and kindness to all, but especially to your friends.

对所有人都要周到善良,特别是对朋友。

It is a good thing to be rich, and a good thing to be strong; but it is a better thing to be loved by many friends.

——Euripides

富有是好事,健壮是好事,被很多朋友喜爱更是好事。

——欧里庇得斯

Friends are relatives you make for yourself.

——Eustache Deschamps

朋友是你自己找的亲戚。

——欧斯塔什·德尚

The best mirror is an old friend.

——George Herbert

老朋友是最好的镜子。

——乔治·赫伯特

Time makes friendship stronger, but love weaker.

时间增强友情,但削弱爱情。

Friendship is a battered old bus, not a bright, shiny sportscar.

友谊是老破车,不是闪闪发光的跑车。

Make new friends, and keep the old. One is silver, the other gold.

结交新朋友,不忘老朋友,新朋友是银,老朋友是金。

The friend is the man who knows all about you, and still likes you.

朋友是对你了如指掌却依然喜欢你的人。

A good friend is your closest family member.

好朋友是家庭中最亲近的成员。

Constant use will not wear ragged the fabric of friendship.

——Dorothy Parker

朋友犹如耐磨的布料。

——道罗西·帕克

Love is blind. Friendship closes its eyes.

——Friedrich Nietzsche

爱情盲目,友谊闭目。

——弗里德里希·尼采

Friendship must be purchased by friendship.

——Thomas Wilson

友谊必须用友谊交换。

——托马斯·威尔逊

There are three faithful friends in life: an old wife, an old dog, and ready money.

——Benjamin Franklin

人生三个忠实的朋友:老妻、老狗、现钱。

——本杰明·富兰克林

Keeping up friendships takes time and effort, but that time and effort is never wasted.

维持朋友关系费时费力,但绝不会白费。

If you knew everything your friends were thinking about you, they probably wouldn't be your friends!

如果你完全知道朋友对你的看法,他们也许不会是朋友。

Be honest; be reliable; be kind; be caring; laugh often. Nothing more is needed in a friend.

朋友只不过是需要你忠厚可靠,和善体贴,常常欢笑。

Try to see yourself through your friends' eyes from time to time; you may see yourself differently if you do.

试着不时地用朋友的眼光看自己,也许对自己有不同的看法。

Often, old friends never seem to look old to us. That may be because they have remained young at heart; or because we, too, have aged, and can't see it in them or ourselves.

老朋友在我们看来好像一直很年轻，也许因为他们心态年轻，或因为我们也在变老，所以看不出双方都在变老。

It is rare to remain in touch with a childhood friend throughout life; but when it happens, it is a great joy.

很少有终生与儿时朋友保持联系的。如果真有这种事情，是非常开心的事情。

True friends do not flatter; but they are eager to praise when praise is due.

真正的朋友不会恭维，但该赞扬时，会毫不迟疑。

Even the best of friends can be jealous of each other sometimes. Don't be ashamed of your jealousy; recognize the feeling as part of human nature, then let it pass.

甚至最好的朋友也会相互嫉妒，不要为此惭愧，认识到这是人之常情，然后忘掉这件事。

A true friend takes pleasure in our talents and strengths; a false friend pretends to.

真正的朋友为我们的才能和力量而感到高兴，虚假的朋友会假装高兴。

A friend is someone you can talk things over with, knowing you can trust them to keep your secrets safe.

朋友是可以与之谈心里话的人,你知道他们值得信赖,不会说出你的秘密。

There is nothing better than the encouragement of a good friend.

——Katherine Hathaway

得到朋友的鼓励是再好不过的事情了。

——凯瑟琳·海瑟薇

A bosom friend afar brings a distant land near.

海内存知己,天涯若比邻。

If you look after your friends, chances are, they'll look after you.

你关照朋友,他们很有可能照顾你。

It is not what you give your friend, but what you are willing to give him that determines the quality of friendship.

——Mary Dixon Thayer

不是你给朋友什么，而是你愿意给朋友什么决定了友谊的质量。

——玛丽·狄克逊·萨尔

A smile is a curve that sets a lot of things straight.

相逢一笑泯恩仇。

Even reckoning makes long friends.

公平算账，友情长存。

Count your joys instead of your woes. Count your friends instead of your foes.

历数你的欢乐而不是悲哀；历数你的朋友而不是敌人。

A hedge between keeps friendship green.

保持距离，友谊长青。

He that lies down with dogs must rise up with fleas.

近朱者赤，近墨者黑。

Birds of a feather flock together.

物以类聚。

A man is known by the company he keeps.

察其友，知其人。

A thousand cups of wine do not suffice when true friends meet, but half a sentence is too much when there is no meeting of minds.

酒逢知己千杯少，话不投机半句多。

It is easier to forgive an enemy than to forgive a friend.

——William Blake

原谅敌人易，原谅朋友难。

——威廉·布莱克

We should behave to our friends as we would wish our friends behave to us.

——Aristotle

我们对待朋友应像我们期待朋友对待我们一样。

——亚里士多德

The friendship that can cease has never been real.

——Saint Jerome

可以中止的友谊从来就没有真诚过。

——圣杰罗姆

True friendship foresees the needs of others rather than proclaim its own.

——A. Maurois

真正的朋友总是先看到别人的需要,而不是提出自己的要求。

——A·莫洛亚

Trick and treachery are the practice of fools that have not wit enough to be honest.

要诡计、搞背叛,是傻瓜的行为,只有傻瓜才不会待人以诚。

We cherish our friends not for their ability to amuse us, but for ours to amuse them.

——Evelyn Waugh

我们珍爱朋友,不是因为他们能令我们快乐,而是因为我们能令他们快乐。

——艾芙琳·沃

A mere friend will agree with you, but a real friend will argue.

普通的朋友只会随声附和,只有真正的朋友会和你争论。

On the choice of friends our good or evil name depends.

朋友的选择会影响我们名誉的好坏。

True friendship is seen through the heart not through the eyes.

真正的友情用心感受，而不是用眼睛看。

There is as much difference between the counsel that a friend giveth, and that a man giveth himself, as there is between the counsel of a friend and a flatterer.

——Francis Bacon

朋友所给的诤言与一个人自己的主张之间的差别有如良友的诤言与谄佞的建议之间的差别一样。

——弗朗西斯·培根

True friendship is not measured in days or decades.

真正的友谊不能用时间来衡量。

Write down the advice of him who loves you, though you like it not at present.

忠言虽逆耳，但需记下来。

A wise man gets more use from his enemies than a fool from his friends.

——Baltasar Gracian

智者从敌人那儿获得的益处比傻瓜从朋友那儿获得的益处更多。

——巴尔塔沙·格拉西安

He who is the slowest in making a promise is the most faithful in the performance of it.

不轻诺者易守信。

Friendship will not stand the strain of very much good advice for very long.

——Robert Lynd

好建议过多,压力过大,友谊难以持久。

——罗伯特·林德

Friendship is certainly the finest balm for the pangs of disappointed love.

爱情遇挫折,朋友是最好的止痛药。

No matter what accomplishments you achieve, somebody helps you.

——Althea Gibson

无论你取得了多大的成就,都是因为有人帮助你。

——阿尔西亚·吉布森

The great confidence in a friend to tell him your faults, greater to tell him his.

把自己的错告诉朋友是对他信任,把朋友的错指给他更是信任。

There is more than one way to help people but there is only one way to live: help people.

助人之道不一,做人之道却唯一,那就是助人。

Do good to thy friend to keep him, to thy enemy to gain him.

对朋友行善以留住他,对敌人行善以争取他。

Pride increases our enemies, and puts our friends to flight.

骄傲招来敌人,赶走朋友。

To preserve a friend three things are required: to honor him present, praise him absent, and assist him in his necessities.

维持友谊需要三点：当面尊重他，背后赞扬他，需要时帮助他。

Don't abuse your friends and expect them to consider it criticism.

——Edgard Watson Howe

不要辱骂朋友，也不要指望他们把辱骂当成批评。

——艾德加·沃森·豪

Knavery may serve a turn, but honesty never fails.

欺诈或许得逞一时，诚实却是长久之计。

He will not have true friends who is afraid of making enemies.

——William Hazlitt

害怕树敌者交不到真朋友。

——威廉·哈兹里特

Don't make friends who are comfortable to be with. Make friends who will force you to lever yourself up.

——Thomas J. Watson

别交那些让你感觉舒服的朋友,交那些让你不得不上进的朋友。

——托马斯·J·沃森

A man dies often as he loses a friend. But we gain new life by new contacts, new friends.

——Francis Bacon

人失去一个朋友,如同经历一次死亡;而结交一个新朋友,仿佛又获新生。

——弗朗西斯·培根

A friend that you buy with presents will be bought from you.

——Thomas Fuller

用礼物买来的朋友终会被买走。

——托马斯·富勒

Trust not the praise of a friend, nor the contempt of an enemy.

朋友的赞扬和仇敌的轻蔑都不要当回事。

False friends are worse than bitter enemies.

口蜜腹剑的朋友还不如不共戴天的敌人。

Am I not destroying my enemies when I make friends of them?

当我化敌为友时,难道不是在消灭敌人吗?

The best time to make friends is before you need them.

——Ethel Barrymore

交朋友的最好时间是在你需要他们之前。

——埃塞尔·巴里摩尔

Only the person who has faith in himself is able to be faithful to others.

忠实于自己,方能忠实于他人。

Friendship is never established as an understood relation. It is a miracle which requires constant proofs.

——Henry David Thoreau

友谊并非一成不变的关系,而是一个需要不断证实的奇迹。

——亨利·大卫·梭罗

An open enemy is better than a hollow friend.

宁有公开敌人，不要空头朋友。

No matter how good a friend someone is, they're going to hurt you every once in a while and you must forgive them for that.

再好的朋友也会偶尔伤害你，一定不要耿耿于怀。

A willing helper does not wait until he is asked.

乐于助人者总是主动帮助别人。

An ounce of blood is worth more than a pound of friendship.

亲情浓于友情。

The holy passion of friendship is of so sweet and steady and loyal and enduring a nature that is will last through a whole lifetime, if not asked to lend money.

——Mark Twain

神圣的友谊具有甜蜜、稳定、忠诚、持久的特性，这种友谊会伴你终生，只要不涉及借钱。

——马克·吐温

The friend in my adversity I shall always cherish most. I can better trust those who helped to relieve the gloom of my dark hours than those who are so ready to enjoy with me the sunshine of my prosperity.

——Ulysses S. Grant

患难朋友最值得我永远珍惜。相对于准备和我一起享受幸福阳光的人来说,我更信任帮助我走出黑暗的人。

——尤利西斯·S·格兰特

Friendship is the source of the greatest pleasures, and without friends even the most agreeable pursuits become tedious.

——St. Thomas Aquinas

友谊是快乐的源泉。没有朋友,即使最美好的追求都会变得索然无趣。

——圣·托马斯·阿奎奈

A friend is someone who, upon seeing another friend in immense pain, would rather be the one experiencing the pain than to have to watch their friend suffer.

真正的朋友在看到朋友非常痛苦时,宁愿自己忍受也不愿看着朋友痛苦。

Keep a fair-sized cemetery in your back yard, in which to bury the faults of your friends.

——Henry Ward Beecher

在你的后院留出一大块墓地来埋葬朋友的缺点。

——亨利·沃德·比彻

Friendship is a horizon—which expands whenever we approach it.

——E. R. Hazlip

友谊是一条地平线——我们无论何时接近它,它都会延伸。

——E·R·哈兹里普

Be slow in choosing a friend, slower in changing.

选择朋友要慎重,更换朋友更应慎重。

When you make new friends, don't forget the old ones.

有了新朋,勿忘旧友。

There can be no friendship where there is no freedom. Friendship loves a free air, and will not be fenced up in straight and narrow enclosures.

——William Penn

没有自由就没有友谊。友谊喜欢自由的氛围,不愿被束缚在笔直狭窄的空间内。

——威廉·佩恩

Become passionate. Love your family, your boss, your coworkers, your friends, and even strangers.

要充满热情,要爱家人、老板、同事、朋友,甚至陌生人。

A true friend is someone you can disagree with and still your remain friends. For if not, they weren't true friends in the first place.

——Sandy Ratliff

真正的朋友是即使有分歧也依然与你保持朋友关系的人。否则,一开始就做不成真正的朋友。

——珊蒂·拉特利弗

True friendship is felt, not said.

——Mariecris Madayag

真正的友谊在感觉而非在语言。

——马利克里斯·麦德雅戈

True friends are hard to find, difficult to leave, and impossible to forget.

——Amanda Kunkle

挚友难寻，难离，难忘。

——阿曼达·坤科尔

Memories last forever, never do they die. Friends stay together, never say goodbye.

——Melina Campos

回忆悠长，无绝期；朋友小聚，不言别。

——麦利纳·坎珀斯

Nations will rise and fall. Wars will be lost and won. Lives will begin and end, but a true friend is eternal.

——Jon Koroluk

国家有兴衰；战争有输赢；生命有始终，挚友却永恒。

——乔恩·科拉洛克

When it hurts to look back, and you're scared to look ahead, you can look beside you, and your best friend will be there.

向后看受伤害，而又怕向前看时，你可以向旁边看，挚友可能就在那儿。

Friends are those who treat you kindly behind your back.

朋友是在你背后善待你的人。

Suspicion is the poison of friendship.

——St. Augustine

猜疑是友谊的毒药。

——圣奥古斯丁

Never deceive a friend.

——Hipparchus

切勿欺骗朋友。

——喜帕恰斯

Never do a wrong thing to make a friend or to keep one.

——Robert E. Lee

不要为结交朋友而做错事,也不要做错事去留住友情。

——罗伯特·E·李

A true friend will see you through when others see that you are through.

真正的朋友在别人认为你不再有价值时,一直伴在你左右。

Often we have no time for our friends but all the time in the world for our enemies.

——Leon Uris

我们常常没有时间给朋友，但对于敌人我们总有时间。

——利昂·乌里斯

A false friend and a shadow, attend only while the sun shines.

虚假的朋友就像影子，只有当太阳照耀时才伴随在你身边。

An open foe may prove a curse; but a pretended friend is worse.

公开的敌人是祸害，虚假的朋友则更坏。

Finding a good friend is an extraordinary piece of luck in life, and one that we should never take for granted. It's important to realize that friendships, like all relationships, must be nurtured; small acts, like helping out with chores, remembering birthdays, wishing good luck for important new challenges, and so on, are all ways of showing your friends that you care.

找到一个好朋友是人生特别幸运的事情，不要认为是理所当然的事情。必须意识到友谊与所有关系一样必须培育，做一些小事情，如帮点忙，记着生日，在朋友遇到重要新挑战时送去祝愿等都是向朋友表示关心。

A true friend is the best possession.

真诚的朋友是最宝贵的财富。

The gift of friendship is the greatest gift a person can ever possess.

友谊是人能够得到的最重要的礼物。

Take care of your friends, and your friends will take care of you.

关心朋友，朋友也会关心你。

Friendship is a sheltering tree.

——Samuel Taylor Coleridge

朋友可以遮阴蔽日。

——塞缪尔·泰勒·柯勒律治

Friendship without self-interest is one of the rare and beautiful things in life.

——James Francis Byrnes

没有私利的友情是生命中少见而又美好的事物之一。

——詹姆斯·弗朗西斯·伯恩斯

There is no formula for friendship, because all friendships are different.

友谊没有模式,所有的友谊都不同。

In friendship, quality is more important than number.

在友谊的问题上,质量比数量更重要。

There are many kinds of love, but the three greatest are: romantic love, the love of a parent for a child, and the love between friends.

爱有很多种,但是最伟大的三种爱是浪漫之爱、父母之爱、朋友之爱。

Your family is given to you by destiny; your friends, by chance.

家庭是命中注定的,朋友是偶然得来的。

Only a life lived for others is worth living.

——Albert Einstein

为别人而活着,生命才有价值。

——阿尔伯特·爱因斯坦

Some friends come and go like a season. Others are arranged in our lives for good reason.

——Sharita Gadison

有些朋友来来去去犹如季节,而有些朋友理当纳入我们的生活。

——沙丽塔·盖蒂森

Prosperity makes friends, adversity tries them.

富贵结朋友,患难见真情。

Friendships multiply joys and divide griefs.

——H. G. Bohn

友谊使欢乐加倍,使痛苦减半。

——H·G·包恩

Books and friends should be few but good.

图书与朋友都应该少而精。

Everyone hears what you say. Friends listen to what you say. Best friends listen to what you don't say.

人人听你说话，朋友倾听你说的话，而挚友听到你没有说出的话。

A race is just a race, but a friend who paces you is a friend for life.

比赛就是比赛，而为你带跑的朋友是你一生的朋友。

Friendship should be more than biting time can sever.

——T. S. Eliot

时间再锐利也切不断友谊。

——T · S · 艾略特

One friend in a lifetime is much, two are many, three are hardly possible.

——Henry Brooks Adams

一生结交一个朋友不少，两个算多，三个几乎不可能。

——亨利 · 布鲁克斯 · 亚当斯

The bird needs a nest, the spider a web, man friendship.

——William Blake

鸟儿需要巢,蜘蛛需要网,人需要朋友。

——威廉·布莱克

To lose a friend is the greatest of all loses.

失去朋友是最大的损失。

Friendship demands:honesty, trustworthiness, tolerance, loyalty, care, concern... and last, but by no means least, being able to have fun together.

友谊要求诚实,可靠,忍让,忠诚,在意,关心……最后但并非不重要的一点,是能够一起玩得开心。

The greatest blessings in life are love, peace, freedom, and friendship.

人生最大的福气就是有爱、平静、自由和朋友。

Friendship is a flower that grows in the most unexpected places.

友谊之花开在最出人意料的地方。

Good friends are good for your health.

——Irwin Sarason

好朋友有益于健康。

——欧文·萨拉逊

The art of friendship is like any other art: it must be practised with love, care, and tenderness if it is to thrive.

交友艺术如同其他艺术一样,必须用爱、关心和柔情使其发展。

A true friend is someone you can trust implicitly, at all times.

真正的朋友是你自始至终信赖的人。

Friendship is love for its own sake.

友谊就是无缘由的爱。

A brother is a friend God gave you; a friend is a brother your heart chose for you.

兄弟是上帝赐给你的朋友;而朋友是你的心为你选择的兄弟。

Fire is the test of gold, adversity friendship.

烈火试真金，苦难试友情。

Perhaps the most delightful friendships are those in which there is much agreement, much disputation, and yet more personal liking.

——George Eliot

常达共识，常争执，更多的共同喜好也许是最令人愉悦的友情。

——乔治·艾略特

Don't walk in front of me; I may not follow. Don't walk behind me; I may not lead. Just walk beside me and be my friend.

——Albert Camus

不要走在我前面，我不一定会追随。不要走在我的后面，我不一定会带路。就走在我的旁边，成为我的朋友。

——艾伯特·卡缪

Do not save your loving speeches for your friends till they are dead. Do not write them on their tombstones, speak them rather now instead.

——Anna Cummins

不要把好话留到朋友弥留之际说，也不要把这些好话刻在墓碑上，要说就现在说。

——安娜·卡明斯

No one is the whole of himself; his friends are the rest of him.

人无完人，朋友补之。

No road is long with good company.

途有好伴，不觉路远。

When friends stop being frank and useful to each other, the whole world loses some of its radiance.

当朋友不再坦率，不再彼此相助，整个世界会为此而暗淡无光。

Friendship is love with understanding.

友谊就是爱和理解。

Love is all very well in its way, but friendship is much higher.

爱情诚美好，友谊更可贵。

A true friend is the greatest of all blessings, and the one that we take the least care of all to acquire.

——La Rockefoucauld

真正的朋友是最宝贵的财富,而我们却无须为获此财富而费尽心机。

——拉罗什富科

The worst solitude is to be destitute of sincere friendship.

——Francis Bacon

最大的孤独莫过于缺乏真诚的友情。

——弗朗西斯·培根

Honest may be dear bought, but can never be an ill pennyworth.

真诚代价高,换来即变宝。

A true friend is one who overlooks your failures and tolerates your successes.

——Doug Larson

真正的朋友既不在意你的失败,也不妒忌你的成功。

——道格·拉森

I value the friend who for me finds time on his calendar, but I cherish the friend who for me does not consult his calender.

——Robert Brault

我重视能为我腾时间的朋友；可我更珍爱随时可以见的朋友。

——罗伯特·布尧尔特

A true friend is someone who reaches for your hand and touches your heart.

真正的朋友有难同当,心心相印。

A faithful friend is a strong defense, and he that hath found such a one hath found a treasure.

忠实的朋友是坚强的后盾,找到这样的朋友如同找到了宝物。

He is rich enough who has true friends.

拥有真朋友,可谓真正的富翁。

My best friend is the one who brings out the best in me.

——Henry Ford

最好的朋友就是使我发挥最大潜能和优势的人。

——亨利·福特

Our best friends are those who tell us our faults and help us to mend them.

最好的朋友是指出并帮助我们改正缺点的人。

The most beautiful discovery that true friends can make is that they can grow separately without growing apart.

挚友最美好的发现是人不在一起,依然心心相印。

Best friends are like diamonds, precious and rare. False friends are like leaves, found everywhere.

最好的朋友如同钻石,珍贵稀有;虚假的朋友如同树叶,到处可见。

A faithful friend is the medicine of life.

忠实的朋友是生活中的良药。

The best mirror is an old friend.

老朋友是最好的镜子。

How rare and wonderful is that flash of a moment when we realize we have discovered a friend.

——William Rotsler

意识到发现了一个朋友,那一刻是多么可贵而又美好啊!

——威廉·罗斯勒

A brother may not be a friend, but a friend will always be a brother.

兄弟可能不是朋友,但朋友总是兄弟。

The most precious of all possessions is a wise and loyal friend.

最宝贵的财富莫过于明智而忠实的朋友。

Gratitude preserves old friendships, and procures new.

感恩之心让你保持旧朋,获得新友。

Old friends and old wine are the best.

陈酒香醇,老友情深。

Nothing is better than a loyal friend.

忠实的朋友是无与伦比的。

True friendship lasts forever.

真正的友情地久天长。

One loyal friend is worth ten thousand relatives.

——Euripides

一个忠实的朋友比得上成千上万的亲戚。

——欧里庇得斯

A near friend is better than a far-dwelling kinsman.

远亲不如近友。

A good friend is better than a near relation.

近亲不如好友。

Wishing to be friends is quick work, but friendship is a slow-ripening fruit.

——Aristotle

结交朋友只在一念之间，友谊却是慢慢成熟的果实。

——亚里士多德

A real friend is someone who walks in when the rest of the world walks out.

真正的朋友是在你在众叛亲离时还不离不弃的人。

The making of friends, who are real friends, is the best token we have of a man's success in life.

——Edward Everett Hale

结交真朋友,是我们拥有成功人生的最好标志。

——爱德华·埃弗雷特·黑尔

A good friend is my nearest relation.

好友即至亲。

I look upon every day to be lost, in which I do not make a new acquaintance.

——Samuel Johnson

哪一天我不结交新识,就会认为这一天一无所获。

——塞缪尔·约翰逊

Don't be dismayed at goodbyes. A farewell is necessary before you can meet again. And meeting again, after moments or lifetimes, is certain for those who are friends.

——Richard Bach

说再见时不要沮丧。有分别,才有相聚。无论何时,朋友注定还会再相聚。

——理查德·巴赫

It's better to be deceived by one's friends than to deceive them.

——Goethe

宁可被朋友欺骗,也不欺骗朋友。

——歌德

Some people go to priests; others to poetry; I to my friends.

——Virginia Woolf

有的人去找牧师,有的人去找诗词,我去找朋友。

——弗吉尼亚·伍尔芙

Old wood best to burn, old wine to drink, old friends to trust, and old authors to read.

老柴最好烧,陈酒最好喝,老友最可靠,老作家的书最好读。

In prosperity our friends know us; in adversity we know our friends.

——C. Collins

在顺境中,朋友结识我们;在逆境中,我们了解朋友。

——C·柯林斯

One should always live in the best company, whether it is of books or of men.

人应该总是有最好的陪伴：或好书，或好人。

The death of a friend is equivalent to the loss of a limb.

一个朋友的去世等于失去了一个臂膀。

Friendship is like a glass ornament; once it is broken it can rarely be put back together exactly the same way.

友谊就像一个玻璃装饰，一旦打破，就难以恢复原状。

A life without a friend is a life without a sun.

人生在世没有朋友，犹如生命中没有太阳。

Life without a friend is death without a witness.

没有朋友的生活如同在孤独中死去。

In the end, we will remember not the words of our enemies, but the silence of our friends.

——Martin Luther King, Jr.

最后，我们将记住的不是敌人的话语，而是朋友的沉默。

——小马丁·路德·金

Speak well of your friend, of your enemy say nothing.

赞美朋友,莫提敌人。

No man can be happy without a friend, nor be sure of his friend until he is unhappy.

——Thomas Fuller

没有朋友的人不会幸福,不幸福时才能确定谁是朋友。

——托马斯·富勒

True friendship is a plant of slow growth, must undergo and withstand the shocks of adversity before it is entitled to that appellation.

——George Washington

真正的友谊是一棵慢慢生长的树,经得起风雨的考验,才名副其实。

——乔治·华盛顿

It is not so much our friends' help that helps us as the confident knowledge that they will help us.

——Epicurus

与其说是朋友出手相助帮了我们，还不如说是确信朋友会出手相助帮了我们。

——伊壁鸠鲁

Friends are the pillars on your porch. Sometimes they hold you up, sometimes they lean on you, and sometimes it's just enough to know that they are standing by.

朋友就像门廊里的柱子，有时给你支撑，有时让你依靠，有时知道他们在身旁足矣。

Friends are angels sent down to earth to make good days and help us find our way.

朋友是下凡的天使，带来快乐时光，指引前进之路。

A friend can tell you things you don't want to tell yourself.

——Frances Ward Weller

朋友可以让你正视你想回避的事。

——弗朗西斯·沃德·威勒

Wherever you may be it is your friends who make your world.

无论你在哪里，是朋友成就了你的世界。

Who pleasure gives, shall joy receive.

予人快乐,自己快乐。

The best friend is the man who in wishing me well wishes it for my sake.

——Aristotle

最好的朋友是真心实意祝福我的人。

——亚里士多德

Friendship is the golden thread that ties the hearts of all the world.

——J. Evelyn

友谊是一根金线,把全世界的心连在了一起。

——J·伊夫林

A friend is one before whom I may think aloud.

朋友就是我可以在其面前自言自语的人。

A friend is a present which you give yourself.

——R. L. Stevenson

朋友是你送给自己的一份礼物。

——R·L·史蒂文森

A friend is a second self.

——Isabelle Norton

朋友是另一个自己。

——伊莎贝尔·诺顿

A friend is one who believes in you when you have ceased to believe in yourself.

朋友就是在你已不再相信自己的时候依然相信你的人。

A true friend sticks with you through thick and thin no matter what happens.

——Kayla

真正的朋友与你患难与共。

——凯拉

Friends are like melons. To find a good one, you must a hundred try.

——Claude Mermet

朋友像甜瓜,要找一个中意的,须尝试一百个。

——克劳德·墨美特

A friend is a person who knows all about you—and still likes you.

——Elbert Hubbard

朋友就是了解你的一切还一如既往喜欢你的人。

——艾尔伯特·哈伯德

The best things in life are never rationed. Friendship, loyalty, love, do not require coupons.

生命中最美好的事情从不定量配给。友谊、忠诚、爱情不需要配给券。

Even the best of friends face conflicts, but that needn't mean the end of the relationship.

最好的朋友也会有冲突,但那并不意味着友谊的结束。

Friends are born, not made.

——Henry Adams

朋友可遇不可求。

——亨利·亚当斯

Good company on the road is the shortest cut.

良伴同行路不遥。

To the world you may be just one person, but to one person you may be the world.

对于世界来说你可能只是一个人，但是对于一个人来说你可能是整个世界。

Life is partly what we make it, and partly what is made by the friends whom we choose.

生活一部分是我们创造的，一部分是我们选择的朋友创造的。

The difficulty is not so great to die for a friend, as to find a friend worth dying for.

找到一个为其而死的朋友易，找到一个值得为其而死的朋友难。

A friend is one who takes me for what I am.

——Henry David Thoreau

朋友就是接受我本来面目的人。

——亨利·大卫·梭罗

Do not protect yourself by a fence, but rather by your friends.

用朋友而不要用篱笆来保护自己。

The company of a good man is the light of the soul, of an evil man the poison of life.

好朋友启迪心灵；坏朋友毒害人生。

One tree does not make a forest.

独木不成林。

Be slow to fall into friendship; but when thou are in, continue firm and constant.

——Socrates

慢慢缔结友谊；一旦成为朋友，就要坚定不移，持之以恒。

——苏格拉底

Plant a seed of friendship; reap a bouquet of happiness.

——Lois L. Kaufman

种上友谊的种子，收割幸福的花束。

——洛易斯 · L · 考夫曼

True friendship ought never to conceal what it thinks.

——St. Jerome

真正的朋友应袒露心扉。

——圣杰罗姆

The essence of true friendship is to make allowance for another's little lapses.

——David Storey

真正友谊的要诀在于体谅另一个人的小过失。

——大卫·斯多利

Build bridges instead of walls and you will have a friend.

建造桥梁,不筑高墙,你就会拥有朋友。

Value friendship for what there is in it, not for what can be gotten out of it.

——H. Clay Trumbull

为现状而珍惜友谊,不为从中有所图。

——H·克莱·特朗布尔

If all my friends were to jump off a bridge, I would not follow. I would be at the bottom to catch them when they fall.

如果我的朋友要从桥上跳下,我不会跟着跳,我会在他们跳的时候站在桥下接住他们。

Better without gold than without friends.

宁可没钱,不可无友。

Poverty tries friends.

贫穷考验朋友。

The only way on earth to multiply happiness is to divide it.

唯有与人分享幸福，才能使之成倍增加。

The friendship between me and you I will not compare to a chain; for that rains might rust, or the falling tree might break.

——William Penn Treaty

我不会把你我之间的友谊比作一条链子，因为雨水可能使之生锈，倒下的树木可能使之断裂。

——威廉·佩恩·崔迪

Friendship is the only thing in the world concerning the usefulness with which all mankind are agreed.

——Cicero

友谊是世上唯一有用的东西，这是全人类都公认的。

——西塞罗

Think in terms of "we", not in terms of "me".

凡事从"我们"着想，而不拘于"小我"。

It takes a lot of understanding, time,and trust to gain a close friendship with someone.

获得他人亲密的友情需要大量的理解、时间和信任。

A friend is like a teddy bear, always there when you need a hug.

朋友就像一只玩具熊,需要拥抱时就在身边。

Real friends don't mind if, when they call, your house is in a mess. They've come to see you, not your house!

真正的朋友来访不在乎你的家是否整洁。他们是看你的,而不是你的房子。

When you're feeling down about yourself, a friend can remind you of your talents, skills, and everything else that's good about you.

当你感到自己一无是处时,朋友会让你想起自己的才华、技艺和所有的长处。

Feeling that one is loved by a friend gives one a great sense of value, happiness, and comfort in life.

感觉朋友爱你,会有生命的价值感、幸福感和舒适感。

Even the best of friends must allow each other a measure of privacy. If they can't, the friendship becomes intrusive.

再好的朋友也必须给对方留有私密空间,否则友谊就成了干扰。

Your closest friends see not only what you are, but what you could be.

最亲密的朋友不仅看到你现在的为人,而且知道你将会成为什么样的人。

I don't trust people who say they have a lot of friends. It's a sure sign that they don't really know anyone.

我不相信说自己有很多朋友的人,这样说肯定说明他们没有什么深交的朋友。

A best friend is the person who understands you better than you understand yourself.

最好的朋友是比你自己更了解你的人。

Friendships are a little like love affairs. If they happen too quickly, they may pass just as quickly. If they grow slowly, they may last longer.

友谊有点像爱情,来得快,去得快;来得慢,时间长。

Sometimes when we meet a person for the first time, he or she feels like an old friend. That's a good omen for a true friendship.

有时一见如故,是建立真正友谊的好迹象。

It's much easier to turn a friendship into love, than love into friendship.

变友情为爱情要比变爱情为友情容易得多。

We can live without a brother, but not without a friend.

生活中可以没有兄弟,但不能没有朋友。

Friends are kisses blown to us by angels.

朋友是天使给我们的飞吻。

The only rose without a thorn is friendship.

唯一没有刺的玫瑰是友谊。

Friendship is always a sweet responsibility, never an opportunity.

——Kahlil Gibran

友谊从来不是机遇，而是一种甜蜜的负担。

——卡利尔·纪伯伦

Friendship marks a life even more deeply than love. Love risks degenerating into obsession; friendship is never anything but sharing.

——Elie Wiesel

友情比爱情给生活留下更深的印记。爱情可能沦为困扰，友情则可永远分享。

——艾烈·维泽尔

Concern for a friend's happiness will enhance your own.

关心朋友的幸福增加自己的幸福。

Friendship is a sheltering tree.

——Samuel Taylor Coleridge

友谊是一棵挡风遮雨的树。

——塞缪尔·泰勒·柯勒律治

A good man terminates a friendship without rancor.

君子绝交不记仇。

Fate chooses our relatives, we choose our friends.

命运为我们选择亲戚,而我们为自己选择朋友。

He whose hand is clasped in friendship cannot throw mud.

朋友的手扔不出泥巴。

But friendship is the breathing rose, with sweets in every fold.

——Oliver Wendell Holmes

友谊是盛开的玫瑰,每一层都飘着芳香。

——奥利弗·温德尔·霍姆斯

Success has many friends.

成功者,朋友多。

Without wearing any mask we are conscious of, we have a special face for each friend.

——Oliver Wendell Holmes

不像平时有意戴着的面具,我们对每一个朋友都有一副不同的面孔。

——奥利弗·温德尔·霍姆斯

A friend without faults will never be found.

没有十全十美的朋友。

So long as we are loved by others I should say that we are almost indispensable; and no man is useless while he has a friend.

——Robert Louis Stevenson

只要我们有人爱,就可以说我们几乎是不可缺少的。有朋友的人,就是有用的人。

——罗伯特·路易斯·史蒂文森

I would rather have a million friends than a million dollars.

我宁愿有一百万个朋友,而不是一百万美元。

The ornament of a house is the friends who frequent it.

——Ralph Waldo Emerson

一个房子的装饰就是频频来访的朋友。

——拉尔夫·瓦尔多·爱默生

Friendship is a cornerstone of happiness.

友谊是幸福的基石。

When a friend asks, there is no tomorrow.

朋友的要求不要拖。

Without confidence there is no friendship.

没有信任,就没有友谊。

Friends are sunshine in life.

朋友是生活中的阳光。

A friend is never known till a man has need.

需要之时方知友。

健康与财富

When we are well, we often overlook the fact that health is a great blessing; it is only when we become sick that we realize how lucky we once were.

无病时意识不到健康是大福气，患病时才意识到自己曾是多么幸运。

Early to bed and early to rise, makes a man healthy, wealthy, and wise.

早睡早起，健康、富有又聪明。

The paradox of life is that as we grow older in our bodies, we grow younger in our minds, reliving the days of our childhood with a new intensity.

生命似乎很矛盾，身体越衰老，心灵越年轻，最后变成老顽童。

People who cannot find time for recreation are obliged sooner or later to find time for illness.

腾不出时间娱乐的人，早晚会不得不找时间生病。

The first wealth is health.

——Ralph Waldo Emerson

健康是人生第一财富。

——拉尔夫·瓦尔多·爱默生

Growing old is not upsetting; being perceived as old is.

——Kenny Rogers

越来越老并不令人苦恼，苦恼的是让人觉得越来越老。

——肯尼·罗杰斯

A healthy mind is in a healthy body.

——Juvenal

健康的思想寓于健康的身体之中。

——朱文诺尔

A man needs a purpose for real health.

——Sherwood Anderson

有目标的人才能有真正的健康。

——舍伍德·安德森

Bitter pills may have blessed effects.

良药苦口利于病。

Cheerfulness is the promoter of health.

——Joseph Addison

心情愉快增进健康。

——约瑟夫·阿狄生

Diseases of the soul are more dangerous than those of the body.

——M. T. Cicero

心理疾病比肉体疾病更危险。

——M·T·西塞罗

Good health is a corollary of having good habits.

健康的身体源于良好的生活习惯。

Happiness lies, first of all, in health.

幸福首先在于健康。

Activities that involve us in the natural world — whether feeding the birds, stroking the cat, or going for a country walk — help us to feel happier.

接触自然——喂喂鸟儿，抚摸猫咪，乡间散步，会带给我们更多的幸福感。

Regular exercise boosts happiness, especially when performed with others.

经常锻炼，特别是与别人一起锻炼，会增强幸福感。

Being happy is known to boost the immune system.

幸福感增强免疫力。

Bath twice a day to be really clean. Once a day to be passably clean, once a week to avoid being a public menace.

——A. Burgess

一天洗两次澡是真干净，一天洗一次澡也说得过去，一周洗一次只是避免对公共场合造成污染。

——A·伯吉斯

The goal of life is the heart of human virtue and human happiness.

——Ushins

生活目标是人类美德和幸福的核心。

——乌申斯

Health is certainly more valuable than money, because it is by health that money is procured.

——Samuel Johnson

健康当然比金钱更为重要，因为我们赖以获得金钱的就是健康。

——塞缪尔·约翰逊

Laugh, and the world laughs with you; snore and you sleep alone.

——Anthony Burgess

笑，全世界都跟你笑；打鼾，你只有独自睡觉。

——A·伯吉斯

Sickness comes by the pound and goes away by the ounce.

病来如山倒，病去如抽丝。

Physicians of all men are most happy; most good success so ever they have the world proclaimth, and what faults they commit, the earth coverth.

——Francis Quarles

世界上最幸福的人莫过于医生；他们的丰功伟绩为世人称颂，而他们的过失则被黄土掩埋。

——弗朗西斯·夸尔斯

The love of beauty is an essential part of all healthy human nature.

——John Ruskin

爱美是健康人天性的重要组成部分。

——约翰·罗斯金

The joyfulness of a man prolongeth his days.

——Apocrypha

快乐使人长寿。

——阿波克拉弗

If we can turn our mind to happiness, love, hope and laughter, we will often find the reward of good physical health.

让心充满幸福、爱意、希望和欢乐,往往会得到健康的回报。

Teaching yourself to be joyful is the single greatest thing you could do to enhance your health.

——Vic Lebouthillier

要改善健康,学会快乐是最有效的方法。

——维克·列布提里耶

Happiness is good for you. It produces endorphins, natural chemicals that act as painkillers.

幸福感有益于健康，会让人体产生一种叫安多芬的化学成分，能够止痛。

Sleeping soundly, and waking refreshed, is one of life's blessings.

睡得香，醒来爽，人生之幸也。

Nobody grows old merely by living a number of years. We grow old by deserting our ideals. Years may wrinkle the skin, but to give up enthusiasm wrinkles the soul.

人老不在年龄；放弃理想，岁月催人老；保持热情，人老心灵依然年轻。

Our three primary negative emotions—fear, anger and sadness—have devastating effects on our bodies when experienced in a prolonged state.

——Vic Lebouthillier

人的三种主要的消极情绪——忧、怒、悲，若长期无法摆脱，会给身体带来致命的伤害。

——维克·列布提里耶

One of the symptoms of approaching nervous breakdown is the belief that one's work is terribly important, and that to take a holiday would bring all kinds of disaster. If I were a medical man, I should prescribe a holiday to many patients who considered their work important.

——Bertrand Russell

神经即将崩溃的症状之一是相信自己的工作极其重要，休假将会带来种种灾难。如果我是医生，我给这种病人开的药方是：休假。

——伯特兰·罗素

The first condition of happiness is health.

—— Curtis

幸福的首要条件是健康。

——柯蒂斯

Health is the thing that makes you feel that now is the best time of the year.

——Franklin Pierce Adams

健康是这样的东西：它使你感到现在是一年之中最好的时光。

——富兰克林·皮尔斯·亚当斯

Without health no pleasure can be tasted by man.
人没有健康,就体会不到乐趣。

Health is better than wealth.

——John Ray

健康胜过财富。

——约翰·雷伊

None so old that he hopes not for a year of life.

——John Ray

再长寿的人也希望多活一年。

——约翰·雷伊

Sickness is felt, but health not at all.

——Thomas Fuller

疾病能感觉到,健康却根本感觉不到。

——托马斯·富勒

It will be all the same in a hundred years.
百年之后,一切依旧。/人生有限,不必事事操心。

Better to be half hungry than ill fed.
宁半饥而不乱吃。

Pain wastes the body; pleasures the understanding.

劳苦伤身，玩乐伤神。

All work and no play makes Jack a dull boy.

只工作不玩耍，聪明杰克也变傻。

A good laugh and a long sleep are the best cures in the doctor's book.

医书上说："开怀大笑、睡一大觉有最大疗效。"

Sleeping is the best cure for waking troubles.

——Cervantes

醒时有烦恼，睡一觉就好。

——塞万提斯

Cares make grey hairs.

忧多生白发。

After dinner sit a while; after supper walk a mile.

午餐后坐片刻，晚饭后走 3 里。

An apple a day keeps the doctor away.

每日一苹果，不用看医生。

There are no such things as incurable; there are only things for which man has not found a cure.

——Bernard Baruch

没有什么不治之症，只是人类尚未发现其疗法。

——伯纳德·巴鲁克

I eat merely to put food out of my mind.

——N. F. Simpson

我吃东西只是为了不再去想食物。

——N·F·辛普森

Life lies not in living but in liking.

生活的意义不在于活着，而在于热爱人生。

The unexamined life is not worth living.

——Socrates

浑浑噩噩的生活不值得过。

——苏格拉底

Life is like an onion: you peel it off one layer at a time, and sometimes you weep.

——Sandburg

生活就像洋葱头：一次剥一层，有时你还得流泪。

——桑德伯格

Life is not all beer and skittles.

——T. Hughes

人生并非只是啤酒和九柱戏。

——T·休斯

Don't believe that winning is really everything. It's more important to stand for something. If you don't stand for something, what do you win?

——Lane Kirkland

取胜并非一切，信念更重要。没有信念，取胜意义何在？

——兰恩·柯克兰

Do not base your happiness on material wealth. It can disappear all too quickly.

建立在物质财富之上的幸福如过眼云烟。

Giving money away makes people feel happier than spending it on themselves.

资助比消费更让人幸福。

Leave virtue and kindness to your children instead of property —only this can bring happiness to them.

——Ludwig van Beethoven

把美德、善行传给孩子，而非财富，唯有如此才能给他们带来幸福。

——路德维希·范·贝多芬

True treasure is simply the love and joy found in you and me.

真正的财富不过是你我心中的爱与乐。

To fail in business is misfortune, but to fail in life is tragic

生意失败是不幸，生活失败是悲剧。

That man is richest whose pleasures are cheapest.

最容易快乐的人最富有。

Happiness isn't about what happens to us, it's about how we perceive what happens to us. It's the knack of finding a positive for every negative, and viewing a setback as a challenge. It's not wishing for what we don't have, but enjoying what we do possess.

——Lynn Peters

幸福不是取决于我们生活中发生了什么事——它取决于如何看待所发生的事。化消极为积极,视挫折为挑战,这就是妙诀。幸福不是祈求所缺,而是享受拥有。

——利恩·比得斯

Do not value money for any more nor any less than its worth; it is a good servant but a bad master.

钱不要看轻也不要看重,金钱是善仆,也是恶主。

It is neither wealth nor splendour, but tranquillity and occupation which bring one happiness.

幸福不是源于财富与荣耀,而是源于心静与职业。

Happiness rarely keeps company with an empty stomach.

饥肠辘辘,难言幸福。

We have no more right to consume happiness without producing it than to consume wealth without producing it.

——George Bernard Shaw

正像我们无权只享受财富而不创造财富一样，我们也无权只享受幸福而不创造幸福。

——乔治·萧伯纳

Yearning for the interests of fiction, is often lost happiness.

—— Aesop

渴望得到虚妄的利益，往往失去幸福。

——伊索

Departure from nature is also a departure from happiness.

—— Jose Johnson

离开自然也即离开幸福。

——约瑟·约翰逊

Happiness is not in the house of gold.

——Balzac

黄金屋里无幸福。

——巴尔扎克

When neither their property nor their honour is touched, the majority of men live content.

财产与荣誉不受损，大多数人都会心满意足。

Happiness is a gift that cannot be bought.
幸福是金钱无法换来的。

There are two ways to attain happiness, get rid of your desire or accumulate your fortune.

——Benjamin Franklin

有两种办法获得幸福：放弃欲望或者积累财富。

——本杰明·富兰克林

A rich man is one who has no need of wealth.
对财富没有需求的人才是富翁。

Women and wine, game and deceit, make the wealth small and the wants great.
女人与美酒、赌博与欺诈使财富减少，欲望增强。

Interest which blinds some people enlightens others.
利益蒙蔽了一些人的眼睛，让另外一些人心明眼亮。

Beware of little expenses; a small leak will sink a great ship.

小开支不可随意，小漏洞会沉大船。

He who multiplies riches multiplies cares.
聚财亦聚忧。

Light gains, heavy purses.
慢慢积累，钱袋沉坠。

Industry, perseverance, and frugality, make fortune yield.
勤劳、坚韧和节俭会给你带来财富。

Content and riches seldom meet together, riches take thee, contentment I had rather.
满意和财富难以兼得，你要财富吧，我要满意。

Money and man a mutual friendship show: man makes false money, money makes man so.
钱和人相互为友：人叫钱虚，钱让人虚。

Avoid dishonest gain: no price can recompense the pangs of vice.
拒绝不正当的利益，作恶的痛苦无法用金钱弥补。

Pay what you owe, and you'll know what's your own.

付清所欠下的债,方知什么是自己的。

The use of money is all the advantages there are in having money.

有钱的好处,尽在用钱中。

Wealth is not his that has it, but his that enjoys it.

拥有的财富非属自己,享用的财富才属自己。

He does not possess wealth, it possesses him.

他并非拥有财富,而是被财富占有。

He that is rich need not live sparingly, and he that can live sparingly need not be rich.

有钱人不必节约,节约者不必富有。

All things are cheap to the saving, dear to the wasteful.

对节约者,东西便宜,对浪费者,东西昂贵。

Light purse, heavy heart.

瘪瘪钱包,沉沉心情。

Laziness travels so slowly, that poverty soon overtakes him.

懒惰走得太慢,很快就被贫穷追上。

Bad gains are truly losses.

不正当的所得才是真正的损失。

Money spent on the brain is never spent in vain.

智力投资绝不会白费。

Wisdom in the mind is better than money in the hand.

脑中有知识,胜过手中有金钱。

All the splendor in the world is not worth a good friend.

——Voltaire

人世间虚名浮利不如一挚友。

——伏尔泰

Creditors have better memories than debtors.

——Benjamin Franklin

放债的比借债的记忆好。

——本杰明·富兰克林

If you would know the value of money, go and try to borrow some.

——Benjamin Franklin

要想知道钱的价值,就想办法去借钱试试。

——本杰明·富兰克林

If your riches are yours, why don't you take them with you to the other world?

——Benjamin Franklin

如果财富是你的,为什么不带着一起到另一个世界去呢?

——本杰明·富兰克林

Money is like muck, not good except it be spread.

——Francis Bacon

金钱好比粪肥,只有撒出去才是有用之物。

——弗朗西斯·培根

No country, however rich, can afford the waste of its human resources.

——Franklin Roosevelt

任何一个国家，不管它多么富裕，都浪费不起人力资源。

——富兰克林·罗斯福

Sometimes one pays most for the things one gets for nothing.

——Albert Einstein

有时候，一个人为不花钱得到的东西付出的代价最高。

——阿尔伯特·爱因斯坦

Riches do not always bring happiness.

财富未必永远带来幸福。

Riches either serve or govern the possessor.

财富可以侍候主人，也可以支配主人。

Riches have wings.

财富会飞走。

Riches serve a wise man but command a fool.

财富侍奉智者，驾驭蠢人。

Small gains bring great wealth.

聚小利,成巨富。

When riches increase, the body decreases.

财富增加,健康衰退。

When we have gold we are in fear; when we have none we are in danger.

拥有黄金,经常担心;两手空空,危急之中。

It is right to be contented with what we have, but never with what we are.

——James Mackintosh

享受拥有,明智之举;故步自封,并不可取。

——詹姆斯·麦金托什

Who will not keep a penny, shall never have many.

不积少,不会成多。

Without wisdom wealth is worthless.

没有智慧,财富就没有价值。